GREAT CRICKET MATCHES 1772-1800 THE PLAYERS AND THE RECORDS

compiled and edited by

Keith Warsop

First published in Great Britain by
Association of Cricket Statisticians and Historians
Cardiff CF11 9XR
© ACS, 2014

British Library Cataloguing-in-Publication Data.
A catalogue record for this book is available from the British Library.

ISBN: 978 1 908165 48 0
Typeset by Limlow Books
Printed by City Press

CONTENTS

Cover illustration

Cricket at the White Conduit – unknown artist, date c.1785? The ground at the rear of White Conduit House, Islington, was used by the White Conduit Club, forerunner of the Marylebone Cricket Club, prior to the creation of Thomas Lord's first cricket ground in 1787. Today a small open space and children's playground, Culpeper Park, occupies part of the probable site.

INTRODUCTION

In some senses this book may be seen as a companion to the Association's 2010 publication, *Great Cricket Matches 1772-1800*. It covers the identical period, and it uses the same definition, agreed by the ACS in 2010, of what constitutes a 'great' match. The contents of this book will undoubtedly be of interest to anyone that has already acquired the earlier work.

However, the present volume also stands on its own merits as a contribution to knowledge about this important period. At its heart is a register of every cricketer that appeared in an eighteenth-century 'great' match, with a brief summary of what is known about him. The register assembles much information that has never before been published in book form, including for instance a definite birth date for the prominent cricketer John Small junior, besides shedding new light on many lesser individuals who had previously been little more than names.

The book also includes a record section, complete with ground-by-ground breakdown, covering 'great' matches of the eighteenth century; together with career records for all the players. It concludes with a list of errata and addenda to the previous volume.

It is hoped that this book will help to stimulate interest in a pivotal period in cricket's history.

The help is acknowledged of a number of ACS members including the late Don Ambrose, Chris Amos, Philip Bailey, Colin Battell, John Bryant, Kevin Clement, Peter Griffiths, Michael Holmes, Ian Maun, Mick Pope, the late Philip Thorn, Martin Wilson and Peter Wynne-Thomas; also the published research of Graham Collyer and John Goulstone.

As editor I am, however, responsible for any errors in these pages.

Keith Warsop

A Note on Match Classification

This book takes as its starting-point the 237 matches between 1772 and 1800 classified as 'great matches' by the ACS. The ACS explained its decisions in the preface to *Great Cricket Matches 1772-1800*, to which reference should be made for a full discussion of the issues involved. Much of the classification was straightforward because it concerned matches of types that are considered first-class to this day — representative, inter-county and between select elevens — but there follows a brief summary of issues concerning other teams.

Berkshire: See under Oldfield/Berkshire.

Brighton: This team enjoyed a fleeting presence in great matches — one game in 1791 and five in 1792 — but the results are good and the matches are included.

Chertsey: Although clearly the leading club in Surrey at this period, Chertsey is significantly weaker than the county side and its matches are generally excluded from the ACS list. However, the 1778 match v England (barring Hampshire) is a special case. Chertsey fields virtually a full Surrey team (Thomas White, of Reigate, is the only major absentee) and England also includes some outstanding players alongside some lesser lights so this particular Chertsey match is included.

East Kent v West Kent: There are eight matches in this category, some of which are billed as matches between the various sponsors, the Duke of Dorset, Sir Horatio Mann or Stephen Amherst. Although the majority of the players involved are from Kent, the teams are reinforced by a number of leading cricketers from outside the county. Even the lesser players are usually recognised Kent cricketers on the fringe of the county side. They were evidently serious contests, one lasting five days and another four, while a Coxheath game in 1789 was important enough for the England XIII v Hampshire encounter to be suspended to allow players to take part. On balance, therefore, these are included as great matches. Similarly, the ACS nineteenth century list includes two matches, Gentlemen of Nottinghamshire v Players of Nottinghamshire in 1842 and 1844, on the basis that the Gentlemen are strengthened by leading players from outside the county.

Essex: See under Hornchurch/Essex.

Gentlemen of Kent: The founding of the Canterbury Week in 1842 introduced the Gentlemen of Kent v Gentlemen of England match as a regular series, with the away game staged at Lord's. These fixtures were always rated among the most important of the season and though other county gentlemen's matches as a whole are omitted from the ACS nineteenth-century classification, these Kent ones are included in line with contemporary opinion. By analogy, six earlier nineteenth-century Gentlemen of Kent matches v MCC and Gentlemen of England are also included. In four of these, Kent had professional reinforcement, which makes them a close parallel to its 1791 game v MCC; this match is therefore included in the eighteenth-century list. Two Gentlemen of Kent matches against the White Conduit Club in 1785 are excluded as the all-amateur teams are weak and only a handful of the players appear in major matches included by the ACS.

Hornchurch/Essex: This team lost to Middlesex in 1787 as well as in three matches against a combined White Conduit Club and Moulsey Hurst side in the same year. From 1789 it played regularly with reasonable results against MCC teams and met Kent home and away in 1792. Its results in 1793 and the standard of MCC opposition were probably better than at any previous time but ironically this was its final year. It is the most marginal of the teams of the period but on balance its matches against WCC/Moulsey Hurst, MCC, Middlesex and Kent are included in the list.

London: A number of matches involve a team named 'London' but there does not appear to be any organising body or any continuity between them so it is likely that 'London' is a convenient label for what are effectively select elevens. The team in the 1797 match v MCC is significantly stronger than the others, with recognised Middlesex county players reinforced by two good professionals, so it is the only London game included in the list.

Old Etonians and Old Westminsters: Three matches are included, two in 1791 (Etonians v Gentlemen of England and v MCC) and one (Etonians v Westminsters) in 1793. The matches against MCC and Old Westminsters include respectively eight and twelve professionals as given men; while the game against the Gentlemen includes most of the leading amateurs of the day plus two professionals. Similar Old Etonian matches in 1816 and 1817 are included in the ACS nineteenth-century list.

Oldfield/Berkshire: For the four seasons 1792-95 this team, on the whole, held its own against respectable MCC teams and it achieved a remarkable triumph by beating a good Kent side in 1794. During this period it was at least the equal of Middlesex and is included in the list.

White Conduit Club: This club was the forerunner of MCC and a decision on which of its matches to include in the great match list takes account of the quality of the opposition.

White Conduit Club and Moulsey Hurst XI: In 1787 a joint team of these two clubs played and beat Hornchurch/Essex in three matches. The full score of the third of these has unfortunately not been discovered but the other two are in the ACS list. Note that Scores and Biographies calls the team in these two simply 'Moulsey Hurst' but contemporary evidence has established that a joint team was involved and this raises the standard sufficiently to merit inclusion.

Eight matches in the ACS list involve odds, all given to England by Hampshire (once) and Surrey (seven times). These are similar in quality to the England v XVI, XIV or XIII of Kent matches at the Canterbury Festival from 1860 to 1881, which have always been counted as first-class. Only one or two of the records included here were set in these eight matches. The eight were:

June 25, 26, 27, July 2, 1789	XIII of England v Hampshire (Lord's)
September 10, 11, 12, 13, 15, 1794	XIII of England v Surrey (Lord's)
September 16, 17, 18, 19, 1794	XIII of England v Surrey (Dartford Brent)
July 6, 7, 8, 1795	Surrey v XIII of England (Molesey Hurst)
August 10, 11, 12, 1795	Surrey v XIII of England (Molesey Hurst)
August 12, 13, 14, 15, 1795	Surrey v XIII of England (Molesey Hurst)
June 16, 17, 1800	XIV of England v Surrey (Lord's)
August 28, 29, 30, 1800	XIV of England v XII of Surrey (Lord's)

The 237 'great' matches may be considered the eighteenth-century equivalent of 'important' matches 1801-1863 and 'first-class' matches from 1864. In effect, and notwithstanding the changes of terminology from 1801 and 1864, these matches comprise a single canon of top-level cricket extending from 1772 to the present day and it is standard practice to compile records and statistics on this basis.

Indeed, one reason for the decision of the ACS to extend its match classification back into the eighteenth century, thirty years after its decision to start in 1801, was the desire not to chop in half the career details of the players from that period. In view of this factor, it would go against the ACS principle if career records in this compilation were cut off at the end of 1800. Consequently, all career records given here include the post-1800 figures for those cricketers who continued playing into the nineteenth century such as William Beldham and Lord Frederick Beauclerk. Similarly, in compiling eighteenth-century ground records, a note has been included of any post-1800 matches plus any changes these made to the records.

The post-1800 details are based on the matches published by the ACS in its series of match scores with the addition of one in 1802 (Lennox's XI v Leycester's XI at Lord's) which had not been discovered at the time these ACS volumes were compiled. However, the 1803 match between H.C.Woolridge's XI and the Hon. W.R.Capel's XI, originally included in the ACS classification, has since been removed as it has recently been shown to be a Rickmansworth club game; therefore it has been ignored here.

SECTION 1: PLAYERS A-Z

The A-Z follows the formula of the ACS county booklet series by including basic biographical information, where available, on those eighteenth-century cricketers who played in major matches. The list of players has been compiled from the surviving 237 full scores of matches from 1772-1800 that have been classified as 'great' by the ACS. Obviously, most of those playing in 1772 had previously appeared but no attempt has been made to trace their earlier careers as evidence and records are sparse and sketchy. Scores before 1772 are available for only a handful of matches, of which only two, in 1744, involve the leading players of the day.

John Nyren (1764-1837)
His father, Richard Nyren, was the 'head and right arm' of Hambledon in its glory days; John Nyren, however, made only intermittent appearances in top cricket but his celebrated memoir, *The Cricketers of My Time*, published in 1833, provides a vivid insight into the cricket and cricketers of the later eighteenth century.

The format for the players' A-Z entries is as follows: Full name; nickname in quotation marks (an entry applying to just a few players such as 'Lumpy', alias Edward Stevens); pseudonym in brackets and italics; date and place of birth and death (or in some cases date of baptism and burial); where educated (if at a major public school or university); relationships with other cricketers; playing style; major teams played for; and years covered by career. An entry in brackets after a player's name, e.g., Bliss (of Ripley, Surrey), indicates the place associated with the player either for residence or as his club; this entry is used only when a birthplace is unknown. The post-1800 career details, where applicable, are shown separately at the end of the entry.

In the case of noblemen, clergymen and army officers, the highest status they reached is given except where a nobleman was known as a cricketer under one title but later succeeded to another, e.g., Lord Strathavon who later became Earl of Aboyne and then Marquess of Huntly. However, knighthoods are shown even if they were gained after the cricket career was over, e.g. G.East = Sir Gilbert East. An army officer's sequence of promotions, where known, is detailed further on in his entry.

It should be noted that the spelling of surnames was not entirely fixed in the eighteenth century, even among the nobility and gentry. Even an educated, literate individual might not always be consistent about the spelling of his name, while various members or branches of the same family might spell their surname differently (e.g. Paulet/Powlett). It may therefore be that various spellings of a name are found in different sources. We have not noted instances of this in the following list, but examples include Amherst/Amhurst, Bennet(t) (Earls of Tankerville), Capel(l) (Earls of Essex), Marten/ Martin. Where cricketing sources are consistent in preferring a particular spelling of an individual's name, we have used that version.

Where an exact birth or death date is not known, details of baptism or burial (where available) are given. Users should exercise caution in using baptismal dates to calculate players' ages, since it was not unusual for families to 'bunch up' christenings, having two or more children of different ages baptised on the same day to save on fees to officiating clergy. In some cases, therefore, there may be a lapse of some years between a player's birth and his baptism.

In dealing with cricketers so far back in time the proviso 'where known' applies to all details of this entry. Playing styles are in the usual ACS format (eg, rhb for right-hand batsman; rf for right-arm fast bowler; wk for wicket-keeper). 'Underarm' is implicit though not stated for the bowling styles. On the rare occasion where roundarm is involved, this is mentioned.

Some clarification of the titles of the 'major teams played for' is required. Such titles are sometimes highly speculative in this period as a report will refer to 'the Hambledon Club' or 'Hornchurch' when the side is elsewhere called Hampshire or Essex.

To avoid confusion in the A-Z we have always used Hampshire rather than Hambledon; Hornchurch instead of Essex; and Oldfield instead of Berkshire.

The 29 Select XIs are not shown under the name of the team's sponsor but for reference these sponsors were: Hon. Edward Bligh (1 match); Earl of Darnley (3); Duke of Dorset (3); John Gibbons (1); Richard Leigh (9); Hon. Charles Lennox (7); George Louch (2); Sir Horatio Mann (6); Edward Gregory Morant (2); Richard Newman Newman (1); Thomas Assheton Smith senior (2); R. Whitehead (2); Earl of Winchilsea (16); and Lord Yarmouth (1). There was also one match between David Harris's XI and Thomas Walker's XI where it is presumed they were the captains while the two sides were sponsored by others.

The appearances shown under the entry 'Single Wicket' relate only to the 15 great matches of five or six-a-side played between 1772 and 1789, one each season except for 1788 when there were two, and four years during this period when there were none: 1776, 1778, 1779 and 1785. After 1789 no comparable matches of five- or six-a-side were ever held.

George Finch (1752-1826),
from 1769 the 9th Earl of Winchilsea
On his return from fighting on the losing
side in the American Revolutionary War,
Winchilsea became prominent in top cricket
in the late eighteenth century. He was
preeminent as a sponsor and organiser,
although his frequent playing appearances
brought only occasional success.

CRICKETERS IN GREAT MATCHES 1772-1800

ABURROW, Edward 'Curry'. b. 1747, Slindon, Sussex; bapt. 24-3-1748, Slindon, Sussex; d. 6-10-1835, Hambledon, Hampshire. He was a shoemaker and linendraper. Son of Edward 'Cuddy' Aburrow (England v Kent 1744). Rhb.
  Hampshire 1772-82 (44 matches)
ALLEN, W.
  Hornchurch, Middlesex 1787; 1791-93 (3 matches)
AMHERST, Stephen. bapt. 3-2-1750, West Farleigh, Kent; d. 6-5-1814, West Farleigh, Kent. Rhb.
  England, Gentlemen of England, Gentlemen of Kent, Kent, Middlesex, East Kent, West Kent, Select XIs 1783; 1786-92; 1795 (31 matches)
ANGUISH, Charles (*C.Clarke*). b. 13-2-1769, St. George's Parish, Bloomsbury, Middlesex; d. 25-5-1797, Cape of Good Hope, South Africa. Educated: Eton. He held an army commission.
  England, MCC, Old Etonians, Surrey 1789-91; 1794-95 (32 matches)
ANNETT, –.
  England, Hampshire, Surrey 1788; 1790-92 (6 matches)
ASTON, Henry Hervey 'Harvey'. b. 1759, Aston-by-Sutton, Cheshire; bapt. 5-12-1762, Aston-by-Sutton, Cheshire; d. 23-12-1798, Madras, India. He died from wounds received in a duel seven days earlier. Educated: Harrow; Brasenose College, Oxford. Joined the Army 1784; captain 1st Regiment of Foot; Lieut.-Colonel 12th Foot 1793. His father was the High Sheriff of Cheshire.
  England, Hampshire, MCC, Middlesex, Brighton, White Conduit 1791-93 (13 matches)
ATTFIELD, Henry. (contemporary scoresheets often abbreviate his surname as 'Field'). bapt. 4-5-1755, Egham, Surrey; d. 1829, Chertsey, Surrey. He was a sawyer.
  Chertsey, England, Hampshire, Surrey, West Kent 1773-80; 1782; 1788 (20 matches)
AYLING, Robert. b. Cocking, near Chichester, Sussex. Brother of William (Kent).
  Kent 1796 (2 matches)
AYLING, William. bapt. 30-9-1768, Cocking, near Chichester, Sussex; buried 29-10-1826, Bromley, Kent. He was a shoemaker. Brother of Robert (Kent).
  England, Kent 1800 (1 match); 1801-10 (21 matches).
AYLWARD, James. b. c1741, Peak Farm, Warnford, Hampshire; d. Edward Street, Marylebone, Middlesex; buried 27-12-1827, Marylebone, Middlesex. He was an innkeeper. Lhb.
  England, Gentlemen of Kent, Hampshire, Kent, London, Surrey, East Kent, Select XIs 1773-84; 1786-93; 1797 (107 matches). Single Wicket: 10 matches.

BAKER, –.
  Hampshire 1777 (1 match)
BARBER, William. bapt. 17-8-1734, Midhurst, Sussex; d. Horndean, Hampshire; buried 10-9-1805, Catherington, Hampshire. He was a shoemaker and innkeeper. Groundsman at Broad Halfpenny Down.
  Hampshire 1772-77 (15 matches)
BARKER, –.
  Hornchurch 1787; 1789; 1793 (4 matches)
BARRYMORE, Richard Barry, 7th Earl (succeeded to title 1-8-1773). b. 14.8.1769; bapt. St Marylebone Church, Middlesex; d. 6-3-1793, Folkestone Hill turnpike, Kent, in a shooting accident. Educated: Eton. MP for Heytesbury, near Warminster, Wiltshire 1791-93. He was a descendant of King Charles II.
  Brighton 1791-92 (2 matches)
BARTHOLOMEW, William. d. before 1800. Son of Rev. Charles (played for Chertsey 1775, but not in a 'great' match)
  Chertsey, Gentlemen of England, Surrey 1773; 1778; 1789 (4 matches)
BARTON, William. b. 16-1-1777, Finsbury, Middlesex; d. Duke Street, Grosvenor Square, Westminster, Middlesex; buried 7-1-1825. He was an attorney. Uncle of Robert (Middlesex 1851).
  England, Kent, MCC, Middlesex, Surrey 1795-1800 (17 matches); 1801-1822 (21 matches)
BATES, –.
  East Kent 1789 (1 match)

BAYLEY, James. (from Sussex).
Hampshire 1773; 1783 (4 matches)
BAYTON, John. (sometimes as Boyton or Boynton)
England 1776-77 (2 matches)
BEAUCLERK, Rev. Lord Frederick. b. 8-5-1773, St George's, Hanover Square, Westminster, Middlesex; d. 22-4-1850; Grosvenor Street, Westminster, Middlesex; buried Winchfield, Hampshire, where he was Lord of the Manor. Educated: private tuition; Trinity College, Cambridge 1790-92. Father of A.F.J. (MCC 1837) and C.W. (Oxford U 1836); son of 5th Duke of St Albans; grandfather of C.S.; uncle of Lord Burford. Ordained 1795, priest 1797. Vicar of Kimpton, Herts. 1797-1827; Vicar of Redbourn, Herts. 1827-50; Vicar of St Michael's, St Albans 1827-50. President of MCC 1826. Rhb; rs.
England, MCC, Middlesex, Select XIs, Surrey 1791; 1795-98; 1800 (31 matches); 1801-1825 (98 matches)
BEDSTER, William. b. 1734, Walburton, Chichester, Sussex; d. c1805. He was butler to the 4th Earl of Tankerville and also an innkeeper.
Chertsey, England, Hampshire, Kent, MCC, Middlesex, Old Etonians, Surrey, Brighton, West Kent, Select XIs 1777-84; 1786-87; 1789-94 (59 matches). Single Wicket: 4 matches.
BEESTON, John (sometimes given as James) (*J.Brown*). bapt. 17-9-1778, London. Related to R. (Middlesex) and William (Middlesex).
England, London, Middlesex, Select XIs 1794-97; 1799 (7 matches); 1804-1808 (3 matches)
BEESTON, R (*R.Brown*). Related to John (Middlesex) and William (Middlesex).
Middlesex 1790 (1 match)
BEESTON, William (*W.Brown*). Related to John (Middlesex) and R. (Middlesex).
England, Middlesex, Old Etonians 1790-91; 1798-99 (4 matches)
BELDHAM, George. bapt. 17-5-1758, Farnham, Surrey; d. 1842. Brother of John (Surrey) and William (Surrey).
Surrey 1800 (2 matches); 1805 (1 match)
BELDHAM, John. bapt. 5-11-1763, Farnham, Surrey; d. 1809. Brother of George (Surrey) and William (Surrey).
Surrey 1794-95 (3 matches)
BELDHAM, William 'Silver Billy'. b. 5-2-1766, Wrecclesham, Farnham, Surrey; d. 26-2-1862, Tilford, Surrey. He was an innkeeper and cricket bat maker. Brother of George (Surrey) and John (Surrey); brother-in-law of John Wells (Surrey); uncle of G.Wells (various teams, 1814-21). His signature on his 1787 marriage licence authenticates the spelling Beldham rather than Beldam. Rhb; rs.
Brighton, England, Surrey, Middlesex, MCC, Kent, West Kent, Select XIs 1787-1800 (117 matches). 1801-21 (72 matches). Single Wicket: 1 match.
BENNETT, James. b. c1774/75, Binsted, Hampshire; d. 31-3-1855, Binsted, Hampshire. He was a farmer. Cousin of John (Hampshire). Lhb; lm.
Hampshire 1798 (2 matches); 1803-1805 (3 matches)
BENNETT, John. b. c1777, Kingsley, Hampshire; buried 24-7-1857, Kingsley, Hampshire. He was a farmer. Cousin of James (Hampshire). Lhb; f; wk.
England, Hampshire 1797-98; 1800 (10 matches); 1801-1818 (51 matches)
BERWICK, –.
England, Hampshire, Surrey, East Kent 1779-80 (6 matches)
BEXLEY, –.
Oldfield 1794 (1 match)
BLAKE, –.
Surrey 1773 (1 match)
BLIGH, General Hon. Edward. b. 19-9-1769, Co. Meath, Ireland; d. 2-11-1840, Ditton House, Thames Ditton, Surrey; buried Thames Ditton, Surrey. Educated: Eton. He was in the Coldstream Guards and later commanded the 33rd Regiment of Foot, reaching the rank of General. Brother of 4th Earl of Darnley (Kent); uncle of J.D.Bligh (MCC 1822).
England, Gentlemen of Kent, Hampshire, Kent, MCC, Middlesex, Old Etonians, Surrey Select XIs 1789-92; 1795-98 (51 matches); 1806-1813 (25 matches)

BLISS, –. (of Ripley, Surrey).
    Surrey 1795 (1 match)
BLUNT, –.
    MCC 1792 (1 match)
BOLTWOOD, –.
    England 1778 (1 match)
BONHAM, Henry. b. 1749; buried 19-8-1800, East Meon, Hampshire. Educated: Hyde Abbey School, Winchester; Magdalen College, Oxford 1770. High Sheriff of Hampshire 1794.
    Hampshire 1778 (1 match)
BONICK, –.
    Surrey 1789 (1 match)
BOOKER, Francis. b. 8-10-1746, Eynsford, Kent; d. 13-11-1806, Eynsford, Kent. He was an innkeeper. Lhb; la.
    England, Kent, West Kent, Select XIs 1773-80; 1782-84; 1786-88; 1790 (45 matches). Single Wicket: 5 matches.
BOORMAN, John (or James). bapt. 18-4-1755, Cranbrook, Kent; d. 1-8-1807, Ashurst, Sussex. He was a farmer and carpenter. Lhb.
    England, Kent, East Kent, Hornchurch, Middlesex, West Kent, Select XIs 1772-73; 1776; 1778-81; 1783; 1786-93 (55 matches). Single Wicket: 2 matches.
BOOTH, George (*Long*). b. 1767.
    England, Middlesex, Select XI 1798-1800 (5 matches); 1801-04 (3 matches)
BOULT, Abraham. Related to George T. (Hampshire, Kent, Middlesex) and Zachariah (Middlesex).
    Middlesex 1787 (1 match)
BOULT, George T. Related to Abraham (Middlesex) and Zachariah (Middlesex).
    England, Hornchurch, Gentlemen of England, Hampshire, Kent, MCC, Middlesex, White Conduit, Select XIs 1786-87; 1789-92; 1795 (20 matches)
BOULT, Zachariah. Related to Abraham (Middlesex) and George T. (Hampshire, Kent, Middlesex).
    Middlesex 1787 (1 match)
BOWRA, William. bapt. 1-5-1752, Sevenoaks, Kent; d. 7-5-1820, Knole, Sevenoaks, Kent. He was a farm labourer, then gamekeeper to the 3rd Duke of Dorset.
    England, Hampshire, Kent, Select XIs, Surrey, Brighton, West Kent 1775-84; 1786; 1788; 1791-92 (50 matches). Single Wicket: 1 match.
BOXALL, Thomas. b. Ripley, Surrey. He was a tidewaiter at Purfleet, Essex.
    England, Hampshire, Kent, West Kent, MCC, Middlesex, Select XIs, Surrey, Brighton 1789-1800 (83 matches); 1801-1803 (6 matches)
BRADES, –.
    Oldfield 1795 (1 match)
BRAZIER, William. b. c1755, Cudham, Kent; d. 7-10-1829, Cudham, Kent. He was a farmer. Lhb.
    England, Kent, Surrey, West Kent 1774-76; 1782-84; 1786-90; 1794 (50 matches). Single Wicket: 8 matches.
BRETT, Thomas. b. 1747, Catherington, Hampshire; d. 31-12-1809, Kingston Cross, Portsmouth, Hampshire. He was a farmer.
    Hampshire 1772-78 (32 matches). Single Wicket: 4 matches.
BRIDEN (or BRIDON), – (*Bell*).
    Surrey 1798 (1 match)
BRIDGER, Henry 'Harry'
    Middlesex 1795 (1 match)
BROWN, –. (This is possibly a pseudonym; if so, the player involved has not been identified. He could also be the Brown who played in the immediately preceding match at the same venue.)
    Select XI 1797 (1 match)
BROWNING, Thomas. bapt. 27-4-1774, East Malling, Kent. Brother of William (Kent).
    Kent 1795 (1 match)
BROWNING, William. Brother of Thomas (Kent).
    Gentlemen of Kent, Kent 1791;1795 (2 matches)

BRUDENELL, Hon. Robert (succeeded to title as 6th Earl of Cardigan on 24-2-1811). b. 25-4-1769, St George's, Hanover Square, Westminster, Middlesex (some sources give his year of birth as 1760 but 1769 is believed correct); d. 14-8-1837, Portman Square, Marylebone, Middlesex. Tory MP for Marlborough 1797-1802. His successor as 7th Earl was the Lord Cardigan who led the notorious 'Charge of the Light Brigade' during the Crimean War.
England, MCC 1790; 1792-93 (9 matches)
BULLEN, William. b. Deptford, Kent.
England, Gentlemen of Kent, Hampshire, Kent, Old Etonians, West Kent, Select XIs 1773-84; 1786-97 (113 matches). Single Wicket: 13 matches.
BULLER, Sir Anthony (knighted 23-4-1816). b. 26-7-1780, Morval, Cornwall; d. 27-6-1866, Mary Tavey, Devon. Educated: Westminster 1788-96 (XI 1796). Called to the Bar 12-5-1803; judge in Madras and Bengal; MP for West Looe 1812-16 and 1831-32.
Select XI 1797 (1 match)
BURGESS, John. bapt. 2-8-1772, Bromley, Kent; buried 16-4-1820, Bromley, Kent. He was a shoemaker.
Kent, Select XI 1794-95 (2 matches)
BURGOYNE, Thomas John (*Boyle*). b. 20-10-1775, Middlesex; d. 20-10-1847, Stratford Place, Oxford Street, Marylebone, Middlesex. He was a solicitor. Father of Thomas (MCC treasurer 1866-79).
England, London, Middlesex, Surrey 1797-1800 (7 matches); 1802-1816 (10 matches)
BURRELL, Sir Peter, baronet (knighted 6-7-1781, succeeded as 2nd Baronet 6-4-1787, created Baron Gwydyr of Gwydyr, Carnarvon, on 16-6-1796). b. 16-6-1754, Upper Grosvenor Street, Westminster, Middlesex; d. 29-6-1820, Brighton, Sussex; buried Edenham, Lincolnshire. Educated: Eton; St John's College, Cambridge 1771-75. Lincoln's Inn 1774. MP for Haslemere, Surrey 1776-80 and Boston, Lincolnshire 1782-96. As Deputy Great Chamberlain he presided over the trial of Warren Hastings.
England, Kent, MCC, White Conduit 1787-90 (7 matches)
BUTCHER, –.
Hornchurch, Gentlemen of Kent, Kent, MCC, Surrey, White Conduit 1787-91; 1793 (23 matches). Single Wicket: 1 match.
BUTLER, –.
London, MCC, Middlesex, Select XIs 1789-93; 1795-97 (12 matches); 1801 (1 match)
BUTTERLY, –.
Select XI 1787 (1 match)
BUTTON, Zachariah. b. c1770, West Thurrock, Essex; buried 11-10-1805, Grays Thurrock, Essex. (His name appears erroneously in some sources as Rutton). Educated: Westminster 1782-87; Christ Church College, Oxford. Enrolled at Lincoln's Inn 1791.
Old Westminsters, Surrey 1793; 1798 (2 matches)

CANTRELL, –.
Middlesex 1789; 1791-92 (7 matches)
CAPEL, Hon. Thomas Edward. b. 24-3-1770, Hertfordshire.; d. 3-2-1855, London. Educated: Christ Church College, Oxford; Exeter College, Oxford; Merton College, Oxford. Called to the Bar at Lincoln's Inn 1791. Commander of British forces in Cadiz 1813-14 during the Peninsular War; Major-General 1814, Lieut.-General 1830, General 1846. His father was the 4th Earl of Essex.
England, MCC 1790 (3 matches)
CAPRON, –.
Brighton 1792 (3 matches)
CARPENTER, –.
Hampshire 1789 (1 match)
CARR, –.
Hornchurch 1789-91 (4 matches)
CARTER, –.
Oldfield, Middlesex 1793; 1795 (4 matches)
CHILDS, –.
England, Surrey 1772-74 (8 matches)

CHITTY, –.
Surrey 1800 (1 match)
CHURCH, J.
East Kent, MCC 1789; 1795 (3 matches)
CLAIR, –.
Hampshire 1797 (1 match); 1803 (1 match)
CLARK, Thomas. d. 1801 (before April), Mountnessing, Essex. He was a farmer. Lhb.
Hornchurch 1787; 1789-91 (7 matches).
CLARKE, –.
Middlesex 1790 (1 match)
CLEMENTS, –.
Hornchurch 1787; 1789-90 (5 matches)
CLIFFORD, Robert. bapt. 8-3-1752, Bearsted, Kent; d. 18-4-1811, Bearsted, Kent. He was a wheelwright and innkeeper. Grandfather of William (Kent 1834-41) and Francis Seath (Kent 1849-60). Lhb, rs.
England, Kent, MCC, White Conduit, East Kent, West Kent, Select XIs 1777-84; 1786-92 (71 matches). Single Wicket: 8 matches.
CLIFTON, Benjamin. b. c1774, St Kitts, West Indies. From 1798 physician at St. Kitts. Educated: Westminster 1785.
England, MCC, Surrey 1798 (8 matches)
CODRINGTON, Captain Christopher Bethell. b. October 1764, Dodington, Gloucestershire; d. 4-2-1843. Became Bethell-Codrington on 17-11-1797. Resided at Dodington Park, Gloucestershire. He could be 'Bethell' who played at Lord's in 1798 (not in 'great' matches).
MCC, Select XIs 1797 (5 matches)
COLCHIN, Samuel. bapt. 21-6-1747, Bromley, Kent; d. after 1808. Nephew of Robert 'Long Robin' (Kent 1744).
England, Hampshire, Kent 1773-78 (10 matches). Single Wicket: 1 match.
COLE, J.
England, Hampshire 1784; 1788 (2 matches). Single Wicket: 1 match.
COLLIER, –. (of Canterbury).
Kent 1786 (1 match)
COLLINS, –.
Hampshire, MCC 1791-92 (6 matches); 1809-1810 (3 matches)
COOPER, Captain G.
Surrey 1797; 1800 (2 matches); 1801-1807 (4 matches)
COUCHMAN, –. (of Seal or Ightham, Kent).
Kent, West Kent 1783; 1786 (2 matches)
COURTENAY, William (10th Earl of Devon from 26-5-1835). b. 19-6-1777, Lower Grosvenor Street, Westminster, Middlesex; d. 19-3-1859, Shrivenham, Berkshire. Educated: Westminster 1789-94; Christ Church College, Oxford 1794-98. Called to the Bar 11-6-1799 (Lincoln's Inn). Tory MP for Exeter 1812-26. His father was Bishop of Exeter.
Select XI 1797 (1 match). Played for Bullingdon Club, Oxford, v MCC (not 'great' matches)
COVENTRY, Hon. Thomas William. b. 24-12-1778, Coventry, Warwickshire; d. April 1816. Educated: Christ Church College, Oxford. Son of 6th Earl of Coventry.
England 1800 (1 match); 1801 (1 match)
CRAWTE, John. bapt. 10-12-1763, Frensham, Surrey; d. 7-10-1836, Boxley, Kent; buried 11-10-1836, Penenden Heath, Kent. He was a shoemaker and cricket bat and ball maker, also an innkeeper. Rhb.
England, Kent, West Kent, Surrey, Select XIs 1788-98; 1800 (56 matches); 1803 (1 match)
CROSOER, Henry. b. c1765, Bridge, Kent. He was a linen weaver.
Kent, East Kent 1786-87; 1789-90 (8 matches)
CUMBERLAND, Captain Charles. b. 21-5-1764; d. 12-5-1835. Educated: Westminster 1772-75. Ensign 10th Foot 1781, Lieutenant 1787, Captain 1793 then retired from Army. Son of playwright and novelist Richard Cumberland (1732-1811).
England, Gentlemen of England, Gentlemen of Kent, Hampshire, Kent, MCC, Middlesex, Old Westminsters, Select XIs 1791; 1793; 1795; 1797 (23 matches); 1802-1804 (3 matches)

DALE, –.
Middlesex 1789; 1791-94 (7 matches); 1808-1809 (2 matches)
DALKEITH, Charles William Henry Montagu-Scott, Earl of. (4th Duke of Buccleuch from 11-1-1812). b. 24-5-1772 London; d. 10-4-1819, Lisbon, Portugal. Educated: Eton; Christ Church College, Oxford. Tory MP for Marlborough 1793-96 and 1806-07, Ludgershall (Wilts.) 1796-1804 and Mitchell (Cornwall) 1804-06. Lord Lieutenant of Selkirkshire 1794-97, Dumfriesshire 1797-1819, Midlothian 1812-1819.
MCC, Select XIs 1797 (3 matches)
DAMPIER, Rev. John. bapt. 12-4-1750, Eton, Buckinghamshire.; d. 18-8-1826, Ely, Cambridgeshire. Educated: Eton; Merton College, Oxford 1769-73. He was Rector of Wylye, Wiltshire, and West Meon, Hampshire 1776-1826; prebendary at Ely from 1812.
White Conduit 1786-87 (3 matches)
DARNLEY, John Bligh, 4th Earl of (succeeded to title 31-7-1781). b. 30-6-1767, Co. Meath, Ireland; d. 17-3-1831, Cobham Hall, Kent. Educated: Eton; Christ Church College, Oxford. Brother of General Hon. Edward Bligh (Kent); father of J.D.Bligh (MCC 1822); grandfather of Hon. E.V.Bligh (Kent), Rev. Hon. H.B.Bligh (Kent) and 6th Earl of Darnley (Gentlemen of Kent 1848); great-grandfather of Hon. I.F.W.Bligh (Kent and England).
England, Gentlemen of Kent, Hampshire, Kent, MCC, Old Etonians, Select XIs 1789-93; 1795-96 (24 matches)
DAVIDSON, –. (sometimes appears as Davi(e)s).
England, Hornchurch 1784; 1787 (3 matches)
DAVIS, Sir John Brewer (knighted 28-9-1773). b. c1741, Hawkhurst, Kent; d. 9-11-1817, Albemarle Street, Piccadilly, Westminster, Middlesex. He was a barrister (Lincoln's Inn) and his father was a clergyman. He was also a captain in the West Kent Militia. Member of the committee that revised the Laws of Cricket in 1774.
Kent 1773 (2 matches)
DAVIS, Thomas.
Hampshire 1773; 1776 (6 matches)
DAVY, – (or DAVIE).
Surrey, Select XI 1787-88 (4 matches)
DEAN, –.
Kent, West Kent, Middlesex 1787; 1789-90 (4 matches)
DE BURGH, Hon. John Thomas (J.T.Burke to 1752; from 8-12-1797 13th Earl of Clanricarde). b. 22-9-1744; d. 27-7-1808, Dublin, Ireland. Educated: Eton. Joined Army 1762; Lieut.-Colonel in 68th Foot; Major-General 1793; Lieut.-General 1798; General 1803.
Surrey 1773 (1 match)
DEHANY, George. b. 17-10-1760, Jamaica; d. 1807. Educated: Westminster 1770-78; Trinity College, Cambridge 1778. Lincoln's Inn 1779; called to the Bar 1784. Brother-in-law of Richard Welch (MCC).
England, Gentlemen of England, Hampshire, MCC, Old Westminsters, Select XIs 1789-93 (16 matches)
DENN, Robert.
Hornchurch, Select XI 1787; 1789-93 (10 matches)
DORSET, John Frederick Sackville, 3rd Duke of (succeeded to title 5-1-1769), previously Earl of Middlesex, Baron of Buckhurst and Baron Cranfield; Knight of the Garter 1788. b. 24-3-1745; d. 19-7-1799, Knole, Sevenoaks, Kent; buried Withyham, Sussex. Educated: Westminster 1754. MP for Kent 1768-69. Lord Lieutenant of Kent 1769-97. Privy Councillor; Ambassador to France 1783-89. Son of Lord John Philip Sackville (1713-65), Kent v England 1744.
Kent, England, Hampshire, West Kent 1773-77; 1780; 1783 (23 matches). Single Wicket: 1 match.
DOUGLAS, Hon. Charles (3rd Baron Douglas from 27-1-1844). b. 26-10-1775, London; d. 10-9-1848, St George's Place, Hyde Park, Westminster, Middlesex. Educated: Eton; Christ Church College, Oxford. Tory MP for Lanarkshire 1830-32. Barrister, Lincoln's Inn from 1802.
Select XIs, MCC 1797-98 (4 matches)

DOWNHAM, –.
    Select XI 1795 (1 match)
DREW, Captain John. b. c1764.
    MCC, Select XIs 1795 (2 matches)
DRUMMOND, George.
    Hampshire, Surrey, White Conduit 1787-88; 1795 (7 matches)
DUPUIS, Rev. George. b. c1757; d. 5-3-1839. Educated: Eton; Merton College, Oxford; Christ Church College, Oxford. Rector of Wendlebury, Oxon. 1789-1839.
    Hornchurch, MCC, Old Etonians 1787; 1791-92 (4 matches)

EAST, Sir Gilbert, 2nd baronet (succeeded as baronet on 12-10-1819). b.17-4-1764; d. 11-12-1828. Educated: Queen's College, Oxford. High Sheriff of Berkshire 1822-23. Resided at Hall Place and Shottesbrooke House, both near Maidenhead, Berkshire.
    Oldfield, White Conduit 1786-88; 1792-94 (12 matches)
EAVERS, J.
    Select XI 1800 (1 match); 1801-1802 (3 matches)
EDMEADS, John. bapt. 21-7-1741, Chertsey, Surrey; buried 24-7-1802, Staines, Middlesex. He was a farmer and brickmaker. Brother of William (Surrey 1775)
    Chertsey, England, Hampshire, Surrey 1772-79 (17 matches). He is reported as appearing in matches from at least 1764; an earlier reference (1759) may be his brother Richard.
EDMEADS, William. bapt. 11-4-1753, Chertsey, Surrey. Brother of John (Chertsey, England, Hampshire, Surrey)
    Surrey 1775 (1 match)

FENNEX, William. b. c1764, Gerrards Cross, Buckinghamshire; d. 4-3-1838, Stepney, Middlesex. He was a blacksmith and innkeeper.
    Hornchurch, Oldfield, Hampshire, MCC, Middlesex, Old Westminsters 1786-94; 1796-1800 (79 matches); 1802-1816 (9 matches). Single Wicket: 1 match.
FIELDER, Richard. b. c1758, East Malling, Kent (although this has been queried, and it has been suggested he was born somewhat later, in Surrey); d. c1826, Walton-on-Thames, Surrey, or Gravesend, Kent. He was a horse breaker and trainer, also an innkeeper.
    Kent, West Kent 1790; 1792-1796 (19 matches); 1801 (1 match)
FINCH, John. He was an innkeeper.
    Oldfield, Middlesex 1792-95 (13 matches)
FINCH, –.
    Kent 1786 (1 match)
FISH, Jasper. b. 1743, Sevenoaks, Kent; buried 28-7-1791, Sevenoaks, Kent.
    Kent 1773 (1 match)
FITZROY, Hon. Henry William. b. 13-9-1765, Southampton, Hampshire; d. 19-3-1794, Lisbon, Portugal. Educated: Eton; Trinity College, Cambridge 1784-86. Inner Temple 1783. Son of the 1st Baron Southampton.
    Brighton, East Kent, Surrey, MCC, Hampshire, Middlesex, Old Etonians 1788-93 (41 matches)
FLINT, –. He played for Colts of Surrey in 1789 and was a bowling substitute in one match for Hampshire.
    Hampshire 1789 (1 match)
FOSTER, Francis. b. c1761; d. 19-7-1847, Havant, Hampshire. He was a tanner.
    Hampshire 1789 (1 match)
FRAME, John. bapt. 21-11-1731, Warlingham, Kent; d. 11-10-1796, Dartford, Kent. He was a drayman and innkeeper.
    England, Hampshire, Kent 1772-74 (7 matches). Single Wicket: 1 match. He is reported as appearing in matches from 1749, aged only 17.
FRANCIS, Richard. (believed born in Surrey). He was a gamekeeper.
    Surrey, Hampshire, Kent, Hornchurch 1773-79; 1782-84; 1786; 1788; 1793 (47 matches). Single Wicket: 2 matches.

FRANCIS, –. (he is believed to be a brother or cousin of Richard Francis but no information has been uncovered).
>Hampshire 1775 (1 match)

FREEMANTLE, Andrew. bapt. 22-10-1768, Bishops Sutton, Hampshire; d. 19-1-1837, Easton, near Winchester, Hampshire. He was a carpenter and innkeeper. Brother of John (Hampshire); father of George (Sussex). Lhb.
>Hampshire, Kent, Old Westminsters 1788-1800 (89 matches); 1801-1810 (45 matches). Single Wicket: 1 match.

FREEMANTLE, John. b. 1758, Bishops Sutton, Hampshire; d. 3-8-1831, New Alresford, Hampshire. He was a master builder. Brother of Andrew (Hampshire); uncle of George (Sussex). Rm.
>Hampshire 1780-82 (7 matches)

FRENCH, –.
>Select XI 1790 (1 match)

FUGGLES, James. bapt. 3-11-1740, Brenchley, Kent; buried 4-1-1777, Cranbrook, Kent. (Another James Fuggles is recorded as baptised 15-3-1746 and buried 22-3-1780, both at the same locations as the former).
>England, Kent 1772-73 (4 matches)

GATES, –.
>Oldfield, Surrey 1794-95 (7 matches)

GIBBONS, Sir John, baronet (from 26-11-1814). b. 8-1-1774; d. 26-3-1844, Stanwell Place, Middlesex. Educated: Merton College, Oxford 1791-94.
>England, MCC, Select XIs 1797-1800 (11 matches); 1801 (1 match)

GIBBS, –.
>Middlesex 1787 (1 match)

GIBSON, –.
>East Kent 1780 (2 matches)

GILL, S.
>Oldfield 1792-95 (11 matches)

GILL –.
>England 1772 (1 match). He may be 'Gill, of Buckinghamshire', who appeared as wicketkeeper for All-England against Dartford in 1759.

GOLDHAM, John. b. c1768, Middlesex; d. 27-1-1857, Forest Hill, Sydenham, Kent. Clerk of Billingsgate Market and Examiner of Wine Duties at Custom House.
>MCC, Middlesex, London, Old Westminsters 1791-97 (22 matches); 1802-1812 (4 matches)

GOLDSMITH, John. bapt. 1-4-1766, Hambledon, Hampshire; d. 15-3-1845, Hambledon, Hampshire. Nephew of P.Stewart.
>Surrey 1792 (1 match)

GOODHEW, –.
>Kent 1791; 1794-95 (3 matches)

GOULDSTONE, John. bapt. 20-5-1764, Ingatestone, Essex. The spelling is taken from the baptismal register, but he also appears as Goulstone.
>Hornchurch 1789-93 (12 matches)

GRAHAM, N. Lhb.
>Hornchurch, Kent, Middlesex. London, Oldfield, Old Etonians 1787; 1789-99 (51 matches), 1801 (2 matches)

GRANGE, –.
>Gentlemen of England, Middlesex 1790-92 (8 matches)

GREENSTREET, –. (of Wingham, Kent).
>Kent 1788 (1 match)

GREGORY, –.
>Brighton 1791-92 (5 matches)

GRINHAM, –.
>Hampshire 1798 (2 matches)

GROOMBRIDGE, –.
>Hornchurch 1793 (2 matches)

GROVER, John Septimus. bapt. 18-12-1766, Hammersmith, Middlesex; d. 28-11-1853, London. Educated: Eton; King's College, Cambridge 1786-91. Ordained priest 1798; Rector of Rainham, Norfolk, to 1817; Rector of Farnham-Royal, Buckinghamshire. 1817-53. Vice-Provost of Eton 1835-51).

    MCC 1790 (1 match)

GUNNELL, W. (of Mitcham, Surrey). He is related to J. (Surrey, 1810) – possibly father and son.

    England 1797 (1 match)

HALE, Edward. bapt. 1-9-1764, Hambledon, Hampshire; d. 16-11-1823, Hambledon, Hampshire. Captain, then Major in Hambledon Volunteer Infantry from 1798.

    Hampshire 1789; 1792; 1797 (3 matches)

HALL, W.

    Hampshire 1782 (1 match)

HALL, –.

    Select XI 1797 (1 match)

HAMMOND, John. b. 15-1-1769, Pulborough, Sussex; d. 15-10-1844, Storrington, Sussex. He was a painter, plumber and glazier. Father of Charles (Sussex); grandfather of Ernest (Sussex). Lhb; rs; wk.

    England, Hampshire, Kent, East Kent, MCC, Middlesex, Surrey, Brighton, Select XIs
    1790-1800 (72 matches); 1801-16 (51 matches)

HAMPTON, Harry. b. 1773, Surrey; d. 12-11-1845, Peckham, Surrey. Brother of John (Middlesex, Surrey).

    Surrey 1800 (1 match); 1802-11 (5 matches)

HAMPTON, John. Brother of Harry (Surrey).

    Middlesex, MCC, Surrey 1793-94; 1796; 1798; 1800 (20 matches); 1801-1816 (25 matches)

HARBORD, Hon. William Assheton, 2nd Baron Suffield (succeeded to title 4-2-1810). b. 21-8-1766, Middlesex; d. 1-8-1821, London. MP for Ludgershall (Wilts.) 1790-96 and Plympton Erle (Devon) 1807-10.

    MCC, Surrey 1791 (3 matches)

HARDING, James. Brother of John (Surrey 1809). He was a labourer.

    Oldfield, Surrey 1792; 1794-97; 1800 (14 matches); 1804-1810 (22 matches)

HARRIS, David. b. c1755, Elvetham, Hampshire; d May 1803, Crookham, Hampshire, buried 19-5-1803, Crondall, Hampshire. He was a potter. Lhb; fr.

    Hampshire, Surrey, Kent, East Kent, Oldfield, West Kent 1782-83; 1786-95; 1797-98 (78
    matches). Single Wicket: 5 matches.

HART, –.

    Brighton 1792 (1 match)

HARVEY, –.

    Hornchurch 1792-93 (4 matches)

HATCH, Isaac. b. November 1764, East Peckham, Kent.

    Kent 1786 (1 match)

HAWKINS, –. (of Odiham, Hampshire).

    Hampshire 1786-87 (4 matches)

HENEAGE, Captain Edward. b. 21-7-1775, London; d. 7-10-1810, Lisbon, Portugal. (He is the Capt. Heneage who played twice in 1800 for the Third Regiment of Foot Guards v the Coldstream Guards in Ireland, scoring nine runs in four innings).

    Surrey 1796 (1 match)

HIGGS, –.

    Hornchurch 1789-90 (3 matches)

HOCKLEY, –. (*Rent*).

    England, Surrey, Select XI 1799 (4 matches); 1804-1805 (2 matches)

HODGES, –.

    East Kent 1781 (1 match)

HOGBEN, –. (of Rochester, Kent).

    Kent, East Kent 1781-82 (6 matches)

HOGSFLESH, William. bapt. 11-11-1744, Hambledon, Hampshire; buried 29-4-1818, Southwick, Hampshire.
Hampshire 1772-75 (11 matches)
HOLNESS, –. (of Maidstone, Kent).
East Kent 1781 (1 match)
HOOKER, –.
Kent 1795 (3 matches)
HORSEY, –.
Hants 1788-89 (2 matches)
HOSMER, Richard. bapt. 3-1-1757, Mereworth, Kent; buried 29-4-1820, Mereworth, Kent (believed died at East Malling, Kent).
England, Gentlemen of England, Gentlemen of Kent, Kent, East Kent, West Kent 1780-84; 1786-89; 1791 (18 matches)
HUDSON, –.
Brighton 1792 (1 match)
HUNT, –. (of Odiham, Hampshire).
Hampshire, MCC 1788-89 (4 matches)
HUSSEY, Edward. bapt. 3-11-1749, Burwash, Sussex; d. 4-7-1816, Lamberhurst, Kent. Educated: Westminster 1764-65.
England, Gentlemen of England, Kent 1773; 1786-87; 1789-93; 1796-97 (18 matches)
HYDE, –.
Brighton 1791 (1 match)

INGRAM, Thomas. He was a victualler. Lhb, wk.
London, Oldfield, Surrey, Hornchurch, MCC 1787-94; 1797 (21 matches)
IRONS, –. (he may be the John I'ons said by the *Sporting Magazine* of 1795 to have scored 197 in a match in 1783).
England 1778 (1 match)

JONES, Rev. Edward. bapt. 16-3-1771, Loddington, Northamptonshire; d. 19-7-1857. Educated: Eton 1783-90; King's College, Cambridge 1790-97. Vicar of Greetham, Rutland; Rector of North Kilworth, Leicestershire, and Milton Keynes, Northamptonshire 1821-57.
Select XI 1793 (1 match). He played for County of Rutland in 1814.
JONES, –.
Hornchurch 1787 (1 match)
JUTTEN, Thomas. buried 17-5-1804, East Preston, Sussex, or buried 16-11-1831, Littlehampton, Sussex (possibly a father and son implied here). He was an innkeeper.
Brighton 1791-92 (5 matches)

KAYE, Sir John Lister, baronet (Lister-Kaye from 22-1-1806, created baronet 28-12-1812). b. c1763; d. 28-2-1827. Educated: Westminster 1777-80. Father of G.L.Lister-Kaye (Sussex 1828).
Gentlemen of England, MCC, Surrey 1787; 1791-92; 1795; 1798 (8 matches)
KENNETT, –.
East Kent 1789 (1 match)
KNOWLES, – (*White*).
Select XI 1797 (1 match)

LADBROKE, James Weller. (see under **WELLER, James**)
LAMBERT, General Sir John. (knighted 2-1-1815) b. 28-4-1772; d. 14-9-1847, Weston House, Thames Ditton, Surrey. Educated: Westminster. Ensign 1st Foot Guards 1791, Lieutenant and Captain 1793, Lieut.-Colonel 1801, Colonel 1810, Major-General 1813, Colonel 10th Foot 1824, Lieut.-General 1825, General 1841. Fought with distinction in the Battle of Waterloo.
MCC 1794; 1797 (7 matches); 1808-1810 (2 matches)
LAMBORN, –. He was a farmer.
Chertsey, England, Hampshire, Surrey, East Kent 1777-81 (22 matches)

LAWRELL, James. b. 21-3-1780, Westminster, Middlesex; d. 7-1842, Leamington, Warwickshire. Educated: Eton; Christ Church College, Oxford (matric. 5-2-1800).

Select XI 1800 (1 match); 1803-10 (20 matches)

LAWRENCE, Richard.

Oldfield, White Conduit 1787; 1792-95 (12 matches)

LEER, George. bapt. 1-4-1746, Warblington, Hampshire; d. 1-2-1812, Petersfield, Hampshire; buried Hambledon, Hampshire. He was a brewer. Famous as long-stop.

Hampshire 1772-79; 1781-82 (44 matches). Single Wicket: 3 matches.

LEGGATE, J.

Gentlemen of England 1789 (1 match)

LENNOX, Hon. Charles (from 29-12-1806 4th Duke of Richmond). b. 9-12-1764, Gordon Castle, Banff, Scotland; d. 28-8-1819, near Perth, Ontario, Canada; buried beneath the Communion Table in Quebec Cathedral. He died from hydrophobia after being bitten by a pet fox. Governor-General of Canada at the time of death. Tory MP for Sussex 1790-1806.

Gentlemen of England, White Conduit, MCC, Surrey 1786; 1789-91; 1795; 1797; 1800 (44 matches); 1802 (2 matches)

LEWIS, M.

Surrey 1773 (2 matches)

LEYCESTER, George. b. c1768, Knutsford, Cheshire; d. 5-7-1827, Portland Place, Marylebone, Middlesex. Educated: Eton; King's College, Cambridge, 1786-89. Assistant master at Eton 1792-99.

MCC, Old Etonians, Surrey 1790-92; 1795; 1797-1800 (19 matches); 1801-1808 (31 matches)

LIFFEN, Thomas.

Brighton 1791-92 (5 matches)

LITTLER, John. b. 1764, Essex; d. 1824, Waltham Abbey, Essex.

Hornchurch 1791-93 (8 matches)

LLOYD, Thomas.

Oldfield 1792 (1 match)

LORD, Thomas. b. 23-11-1755, Thirsk, Yorkshire; d. 13-1-1832, West Meon, Hampshire. He was a wine merchant and farmer. Founder of Lord's Ground. Father of Thomas jun. (Middlesex).

Middlesex, London, MCC, Old Etonians 1787; 1789-99 (57 matches); 1801-1815 (3 matches)

LOUCH, George. bapt. 24-11-1746, Chatham, Kent; d. 29-4-1811, Ramsgate, Kent. Educated: Westminster.

Gentlemen of England, Kent, White Conduit, Middlesex, MCC, Old Westminsters, West Kent 1773; 1783; 1786-97 (122 matches)

LUCK, –. (of Strood, Kent).

Kent 1793 (3 matches)

'LUMPY' (see under **STEVENS, Edward**).

LUSHINGTON, Stephen. b. 14-1-1782, London; d. 19-1-1873, Ockham Park, Surrey. Educated: Eton; All Souls College, Oxford. Fellow of All Souls; Judge; MP for Great Yarmouth, Tregony, Ilchester, Tower Hamlets. Great-uncle of A.H. (Hampshire 1877); cousin of Stephen Rumbold Lushington (East Kent, did not appear in 'great' matches).

Surrey 1799 (3 matches); (also for Bullingdon Club and Prince's Plain which became West Kent CC).

MADDOX, J.

MCC 1791 (1 match)

MAITLAND, General Sir Peregrine. (knighted 22-6-1815). b. 6-7-1777, Longparish House, Hampshire; d. 30-5-1854, Eaton Place West, Westminster, Middlesex. Educated: Winchester. Joined Army as Ensign in 1st Foot Guards 1792; Lieutenant and Captain 1794; Colonel 1803; General 1846. Played a crucial role in the victory over Napoleon at the Battle of Waterloo in 1815. Lieut.-Governor Upper Canada 1818; Lieut.-Governor Nova Scotia 1828-34; Commander-in-Chief Madras Army 1836-38; Governor of the Cape of Good Hope and Commander-in-Chief of the Army 1843-46. Father of C.M.B., from 9-10-1815 son-in-law of 4th Duke of Richmond (i.e. the former Hon. Charles Lennox).

Surrey 1798-1800 (8 matches); 1804-1808 (16 matches)

MANN, Sir Horatio 'Horace', baronet. (knighted 1768, succeeded as 2nd baronet 6-11-1786) b. 2-2-1744, Egerton, Kent; d. 2-4-1814, Union Crescent, Margate, Kent; buried Linton, near Maidstone, Kent. Educated: Charterhouse; Peterhouse College, Cambridge 1760-63. MP for Maidstone 1774-84, then Sandwich 1790-1807.
  Kent 1773 (2 matches). Single Wicket: 1 match.
MANN, Noah. bapt. 14-8-1756, Northchapel, Sussex; d. 8-12-1789, Northchapel, Sussex. He died from burns after falling into a fire. He was a shoemaker and innkeeper. Lhb. (SB has birth date as 15-11-1756.)
  Hampshire, Surrey, West Kent 1777-84; 1786-9 (56 matches). Single Wicket: 10 matches.
MANSFIELD, –.
  England 1778 (1 match)
MARCHANT, J.
  Brighton 1791-92 (5 matches)
MARCLEW, –. (His name also appears as Marklin).
  Select XI 1795 (1 match)
MARTEN, Sir Henry William, baronet (succeeded as 2nd baronet 1-8-1794). b. 20-12-1768 Bishopstown, Co. Cork, Ireland; d. 3-2-1842, London.
  MCC 1797; 1799-1800 (5 matches); 1801-1813 (2 matches)
MARTIN, J.
  Hornchurch, White Conduit, Middlesex 1787; 1789-91; 1793 (10 matches)
MARTIN, T.
  East Kent 1781; 1783 (2 matches)
MATTHEWS, –.
  Middlesex 1789 (1 match)
MAY, Richard. b. c1750; d. c1796. He was a yeoman and gamekeeper. Brother of Thomas (Kent).
  England, Hampshire, Kent, East Kent 1772-76; 1779-80 (13 matches). Single Wicket: 3 matches.
MAY, Thomas. Brother of Richard (Hampshire, Kent).
  England, Kent 1772-73 (5 matches). Single Wicket: 1 match.
MAY, –.
  Hampshire 1797-98 (4 matches)
MELLISH, Thomas. b. c1773; d. 29-7-1837, Uxbridge, Middlesex. Educated: Eton 1783-86.
  Middlesex, Old Etonians 1793-97; 1800 (22 matches); 1801-1815 (18 matches)
MILES, –.
  Hornchurch 1793 (1 match)
MILLER, Joseph. (of Caterham, Surrey); buried 20-10-1799, Bridge, near Canterbury, Kent. He was gamekeeper to 3rd Duke of Dorset. Brother of Richard (Surrey, Kent).
  Surrey 1774 (1 match)
MILLER, Sir John Edward Augustus Riggs, baronet (succeeded as 2nd baronet 28-5-1798). b. 1770, Paris, France; d. 2-8-1825; buried in Bath Abbey. Educated: Eton; Christ Church College, Oxford (matric. 15-10-1789). Lincoln's Inn 8-4-1788.
  Old Etonians 1791 (1 match)
MILLER, Richard. b. c1743 (of Caterham, Surrey); buried 31-10-1784, Bridge, near Canterbury, Kent. His career is erroneously attributed to Joseph Miller in S&B. He was gamekeeper to Sir Horatio Mann. Brother of Joseph (Surrey).
  England, Surrey, Kent, East Kent 1772-83 (54 matches). Single Wicket: 8 matches.
MILLS, –.
  Chertsey, England, Surrey, East Kent, West Kent 1778-81 (9 matches)
MILSINGTON, Thomas Charles Colyear, Viscount. (from 15-11-1823 4th Earl of Portmore). b. 27-3-1772, London; d. 18-1-1835. MP for Boston (Lincs.) 1796-1802.
  Hampshire, Surrey 1792-93 (3 matches)
MINCHIN, John (he usually appeared as Minshull). b. 1741, Acton, Middlesex; buried 23-10-1793, Kingston, Surrey. He was gardener to 3rd Duke of Dorset.
  Chertsey, England, Kent, Surrey, West Kent 1772-80 (28 matches). Single Wicket: 3 matches.
MONK, –.
  Oldfield 1792-95 (10 matches)

MONSON, Hon. George Henry. b. 17-10-1755; d. 17-6-1823. Educated: Eton.

    MCC, White Conduit, Surrey 1786; 1788; 1792 (10 matches)

MORANT, Edward Gregory (later Morant-Gale). b. 29-11-1772; d. 2-8-1855, Upham House, Upham, Hampshire. He inherited the Gale family's prosperous and extensive Jamaica sugar plantations.

    Oldfield, Select XI 1793-95 (3 matches)

MUGGERIDGE, –. (of Epsom, Surrey).

    Surrey 1774; 1776; 1778 (4 matches)

MUNDY, –. (of Andover, Hampshire).

    Hampshire 1792; 1797 (2 matches)

MURRAY, –.

    Hornchurch 1787; 1789 (3 matches)

NEALE, J.

    Hampshire 1788-89; 1792 (3 matches)

NEWMAN, Richard Newman. (He changed his name from Richard Newman Harding on receiving an inheritance.) b. 4-1-1756; d. 1-2-1808. Educated: Eton.

    England, Hornchurch, Kent, West Kent, White Conduit 1773; 1780; 1786-87; 1793 (19 matches)

NICHOLSON, –.

    Kent 1788 (1 match)

NICOLL, Rev. Thomas Vere Richard. b. c1770, Oxford; bapt. 2-3-1770, Bodicote, Banbury, Oxfordshire; d. 22-10-1841, Cherington, Warwickshire. Educated: Westminster 1783-86; Oriel College, Oxford 1788. Rector of Cherington from 1796.

    Gentlemen of England, Middlesex, Old Westminsters 1790-94 (12 matches)

NYREN, John. b. 15-12-1764, Catherington, Hampshire; d. 30-6-1837, Bromley-by-Bow, Middlesex. He was a calico printer. Author of *The Young Cricketer's Tutor* (incorporating the celebrated memoir *The Cricketers of My Time*), 1833. Son of Richard Nyren (Hampshire). Lhb.

    Hampshire 1787-89 (4 matches); 1802-1817 (12 matches)

NYREN, Richard. bapt. 25-4-1734, Eartham, Sussex; d. 25-4-1797, Leigh or Lee, Kent. Surname given in a number of newspaper match details as Nyland. He was an innkeeper and baker, also Hambledon postmaster. Father of John Nyren (Hampshire). Lhb; lm.

    Hampshire 1772-84; 1786 (49 matches). Single Wicket: 3 matches. First reported in matches in 1759.

OLIVER, –.

    Middlesex 1787 (1 match)

ONSLOW, General Hon Denzil. b. 12-9-1770, Marylebone, Middlesex; d. 21-8-1838, Huntingdon. In 97th Foot; Lieut.-Col. 1794; Colonel 1800; Major-General 1805; Lieut.-General 1812; General 1825.

    MCC, Kent 1796-97; 1799 (4 matches); 1801-1808 (6 matches)

OXLEY, W.

    Hornchurch 1790-93 (8 matches)

PACKER, –.

    Middlesex 1790 (1 match)

PAGE, –. (John or William of Guildford, Surrey)

    England, Surrey 1772-73 (2 matches)

PALMER, William. bapt. 9-1-1737, Coulsdon, Surrey; buried 8-2-1790; Coulsdon, Surrey. Twin brother of Henry (Coulsdon 1775). Long-stop.

    England, Surrey 1772-76 (17 matches). Single Wicket: 1 match.

PALMER, –.

    Kent, West Kent 1789 (7 matches)

PARK, –.

    MCC 1795 (1 match)

PATTENDEN, Thomas. bapt. 5-1-1742, East Peckham, Kent; buried 10-11-1791, East Peckham, Kent. He was an innkeeper. Brother of William (Kent).
  England, Kent, East Kent, West Kent 1772-77; 1779-83 (30 matches)
PATTENDEN, William. bapt. 31-10-1747, East Peckham, Kent; d. 1817, Hadlow, Kent; buried 2-4-1817, East Peckham, Kent. Brother of Thomas (Kent).
  Kent, East Kent, West Kent 1780-81; 1783; 1786 (5 matches)
PAYNE, T.
  Surrey 1795 (1 match)
PEMMELL, –. (also as Pemell and Pennell).
  England, East Kent 1777-78; 1781 (3 matches)
PHILLIPS, Constantine. bapt. 2-11-1746, Chelsham, Surrey; buried 14-2-1811, Chelsham, Surrey.
  Surrey, England 1773; 1777-78 (3 matches)
PILCHER, John. b. c1765, Kent; d. 16-3-1838, Canterbury, Kent; buried Westgate, Canterbury, Kent. He was a shoemaker.
  Kent, East Kent 1787-96 (31 matches). Single Wicket: 1 match.
PITCAIRN, Alexander. b. c1764; d. 17-11-1814, Eynsford, Kent. Educated: Harrow 1775-80. Lincoln's Inn 1786-94. Called to the Bar.
  Gentlemen of England, Gentlemen of Kent, MCC, Hampshire 1791-92 (9 matches)
POLDEN, –. He appears in a major single-wicket match in 1779 for the Duke of Dorset's team (full score not known).
  England 1778 (1 match)
PRIEST, –.
  Brighton 1792 (1 match)
PURCHASE, Richard. b. 24-9-1756, Liss, Hampshire; d. 1-4-1837, Liss, Hampshire. He was a blacksmith and gamekeeper. Rhb; rsa.
  East Kent, Hampshire, MCC, Brighton, Old Etonians 1773-74; 1781-84; 1786-98; 1800 (113 matches); 1803 (1 match). Single Wicket: 3 matches.

QUARME, Robert. bapt. 15-1-1766, St Martin in the Fields, Westminster, Middlesex; d. 28-6-1842, Harley Place, Marylebone, Middlesex. Gentleman Usher of the Green Rod (1800-42).
  Oldfield 1792-93 (4 matches)
QUIDDINGTON, Thomas. bapt. 21-1-1743, Coulsdon, Surrey; buried 6-12-1804, Coulsdon, Surrey. He was a farmer.
  Surrey 1774-76 (4 matches)

RAY, Thomas.
  London, Middlesex, Oldfield, Old Westminsters, MCC 1792-1800 (59 matches); 1801-1811 (13 matches)
READ, –.
  England 1773 (1 match). Single Wicket: 1 match.
REDETT, C. (or RIDET)
  Surrey 1796 (1 match)
REED, Charles. b. c1771.
  England 1800 (1 match); 1801-1810 (5 matches)
REMINGTON, Benjamin. bapt. 12-8-1753, Boughton Monchelsea, near Maidstone, Kent. Brother of Michael (Kent, Hornchurch) and Thomas (Kent). The name also appears as Rimmington but registry sources confirm Remington as correct.
  England, Kent, East Kent 1779-81; 1783 (13 matches)
REMINGTON, Michael. bapt. 16-12-1757, Boughton Monchelsea, near Maidstone, Kent. d. January 1826, Rochester, Kent. Brother of Benjamin (Kent) and Thomas (Kent).
  Hornchurch, Kent, White Conduit, 1781; 1787; 1791 (7 matches)
REMINGTON, Thomas. bapt. 11-4-1762, Boughton Monchelsea, near Maidstone, Kent. Brother of Benjamin (Kent) and Michael (Kent, Hornchurch).
  England, Kent, East Kent 1780-81 (4 matches)

REYNOLDS, Frederic. b. 1-11-1764, Lime Street, City of London; d. 16-4-1841, Warren Street, Fitzroy Square, St Pancras, Middlesex. Educated: Westminster 1776. Well-known dramatist of around 100 stage pieces, some of which include mention of cricket in the dialogue, who covers his cricket experiences in his memoirs of 1826, *The Life and Times of Frederic Reynolds*. He was included in Byron's 1808 poetic satire, *English Bards and Scotch Reviewers*. Member of MCC.

    England, Select XI 1795-96 (2 matches)

RICE, James (*Smith*).

    Middlesex 1795; 1797 (4 matches); 1811-1813 (3 matches)

RIDGE, Thomas. b. c1737, Kilmiston, Hampshire; d. 3-2-1801, Kimpston, Hampshire. Educated: Westminster 1750; Trinity College, Cambridge 1754-61. JP for Southampton.

    Hampshire 1772-75 (5 matches)

RING, George. b. 9-4-1770, Darenth, near Dartford, Kent; d. 4-5-1865, Bethersden, Kent. He was whipper-in to Sir Horatio Mann, then gamekeeper to Earl Cornwallis, then to Mr Witherden at Bethersden, and later a farmer. Brother of John (Kent, Hampshire).

    England 1796 (2 matches)

RING, John. 'Little Joey'. b. 1758, Darenth, near Dartford, Kent; d. 25-10-1800, Bridge, near Canterbury, Kent. Servant to Mr Mumford, then huntsman to Sir Horatio Mann. Brother of George (England).

    England, Kent, Hampshire, Oldfield, East Kent 1782-84; 1786-96 (89 matches). Single Wicket: 6 matches.

ROBINSON, Robert. 'Long Bob' b. 1765, Ash, near Farnham, Surrey; d. 2-9-1822, Ash, near Farnham, Surrey (or 2-10-1822). He was a gamekeeper. Lhb.

    England, Hampshire, Kent, MCC, Surrey, Select XIs 1792-1800 (52 matches); 1801-1819 (59 matches)

RUBEGALL, –.

    Middlesex 1794 (1 match)

RUSSELL, C. (of Rochester, Kent).

    England 1795 (1 match)

RUSSELL, John.

    Hornchurch 1787; 1790-91; 1793 (6 matches)

SADLER, –.

    Select XI 1793 (1 match)

SALE, –. Educated: Eton.

    Oldfield, MCC, Old Etonians 1791-93 (4 matches)

SAUNDERSON, Colonel Thomas.

    Select XI 1797 (1 match)

SCOTT, Thomas. b. c1765-66, Alton, Hampshire; d. 5-11-1799, buried Alton, Hampshire. He was a glover.

    England, Hornchurch, Hampshire, MCC, Select XIs 1789-95; 1798 (29 matches)

SCOTT, –. (an amateur, not to be confused with the professional, Thomas Scott, above).

    MCC 1793; 1797 (3 matches)

SELBY, Thomas.

    West Kent 1790 (1 match)

SHACKLE, Thomas.

    MCC, Middlesex, Oldfield 1789-96 (26 matches); 1807-1809 (3 matches)

SHARPE, D.

    Brighton 1792 (1 match)

SHELLEY, Sir John, baronet (succeeded as 6th baronet 11-9-1783). b. 3-3-1772, Michelgrove, Sussex; d. 28-3-1852, Fulham, Middlesex. Educated: Eton; Winchester; Clare College, Cambridge 1789. Distant relation of the poet Percy Bysshe Shelley. Ensign in Coldstream Guards 1790, Lieutenant and Captain 1793. MP for Heston 1806, then Lewes 1816-31. As racehorse owner twice won the Derby, with Phantom in 1811 and Cedric in 1824.

    Brighton, MCC 1792; 1794-95 (8 matches)

SHEPHEARD, George. b. 26-1-1770, Guildford, Surrey; d. 7-9-1842, Guilford Street, St Pancras, Middlesex. Educated: Royal Academy Schools from 1786 (silver medal 1790). Artist who drew sketches of cricketers c1795. Exhibited at the Royal Academy 1811-42.
  Surrey 1796 (1 match)
SIMMONS, Richard. bapt. 3-10-1737, Bridge, near Canterbury, Kent; buried 25-11-1802, Bridge, near Canterbury, Kent. Wk.
  Chertsey, England, Kent, Surrey 1772-75; 1778-79 (13 matches)
SIMMONS, –.
  Hornchurch 1790-91 (3 matches)
SKINNER, T.
  Hampshire 1781 (1 match)
SLATER, C.
  Middlesex 1787 (3 matches)
SMALL, Eli. b. 1767, Petersfield, Hampshire; d. 20-5-1837, Petersfield, Hampshire. Son of John senior (Hampshire); brother of John junior (Hampshire).
  MCC 1796 (1 match)
SMALL, John senior. b. 19-4-1737, Empshott, Hampshire; d. 31-12-1826, Petersfield, Hampshire. He was a shoemaker, haberdasher and made cricket bats and balls. Also gamekeeper to Manor of Greatham, Hampshire. Father of John junior (Hampshire) and Eli (MCC).
  England, Hampshire, East Kent 1772-84; 1786-98 (111 matches). Single Wicket: 14 matches.
  First definitely reported playing in 1768, although he must have appeared earlier: "He is said to have commenced his career in great matches in 1755, when only 18 years of age." (SB p.241)
SMALL, John junior. b. 7-10-1765, Petersfield, Hampshire; d. 21-1-1836, Petersfield, Hampshire. He was a mercer. Son of John senior (Hampshire); brother of Eli (MCC).
  East Kent, Hampshire 1784; 1787-1800 (104 matches); 1801-1810 (40 matches). Single Wicket: 2 matches.
SMALL, –.
  Kent 1788 (1 match)
SMITH, James. b. 1772, Shorne, Kent.
  England, Kent 1792-94; 1800 (7 matches)
SMITH, Thomas Assheton senior. (born Thomas Assheton, he assumed the surname Smith following an inheritance). b. c1752; d. 12-5-1828, Tidworth House, Wiltshire. Educated: Eton. MP for Caernarvonshire 1774-80 and Andover 1797-1821. Sheriff of Caernarvonshire 1783-84; Lord Lieutenant of Caernarvonshire 1822-28. Father of Thomas Assheton junior (Surrey).
  Hampshire, MCC, Old Etonians 1787-94 (43 matches)
SMITH, Thomas Assheton junior. b. 2-8-1776, Queen Anne Street, Cavendish Square, Marylebone, Middlesex; d. 9-9-1858, Vaynol Park, Bangor, Caernarvonshire; buried Tidworth, Wiltshire. Educated: Eton 1783-93 (XI 1793); Christ Church College, Oxford 1794. MP for Andover 1821-31 and Caernarvonshire 1832-41. Son of T.A. senior (Hampshire, MCC).
  Surrey 1798 (3 matches); 1802-1820 (37 matches)
SOANE, –.
  England 1795 (2 matches)
SPENCER, –.
  Hornchurch 1793 (1 match)
STANFORD, Richard. bapt. 21-6-1754, East Peckham, Kent; d. 16-7-1792.
  England, Kent, East Kent, West Kent 1780-81; 1783; 1786-87 (8 matches)
STANHOPE, –.
  Middlesex, MCC 1787; 1789; 1798 (6 matches)
STEVENS, Edward. 'Lumpy'. b. c1735, Send, Surrey; d. 7-9-1819, Walton-on-Thames, Surrey. He was gardener to the 4th Earl of Tankerville. First definitely reported playing in 1769, although he is very likely to have appeared earlier.
  Chertsey, England, Surrey, Kent, Hampshire, West Kent 1772-84; 1786-89 (83 matches). Single Wicket: 5 matches.
STEVENS, John. b. c1769; South Ockenden, Essex; d. 13-1-1863, Hornchurch, Essex. He was a farmer.
  Hornchurch 1789-93 (11 matches)

STEVENS, Very Rev. Robert. (*R.Stone*) b. 1777, Botesdale, Suffolk; d. 3-2-1870, The Deanery, Rochester, Kent. Educated: Westminster 1793-96 (XI 1796); Trinity College, Cambridge 1797-1801. Ordained 1801, priest 1802, Rector of St James's, Garlickhithe, London, 1814-21, Prebendary Lincoln 1814-70, Chaplain of House of Commons 1816, Dean of Rochester 1820-70, Vicar of West Farleigh, Kent, 1820-70.

    England, MCC, Select XI 1797; 1799 (3 matches)

STEWART, Henry. bapt. 5-8-1763, Hambledon, Hampshire; d. 12-3-1837, Hambledon, Hampshire. Brother of John (Hampshire), nephew of Peter.

    Hampshire 1788-89 (2 matches)

STEWART, John. bapt. 6-5-1768, Hambledon, Hampshire; d. 1837, Hambledon, Hampshire. He was an innkeeper. Brother of Henry (Hampshire).

    Hampshire 1792; 1797 (2 matches); 1806 (1 match)

STEWART, Peter 'Buck'. bapt. 26-7-1730, Hambledon, Hampshire; buried 15-2-1796, Hambledon, Hampshire. He was a carpenter, shoemaker and innkeeper. Uncle of Henry, John and J.Goldsmith.

    Hampshire 1772-74; 1776; 1778-79 (16 matches). First definitely reported playing in 1764, but very likely to have appeared earlier.

STEWART, R.

    Gentlemen of England, MCC 1791-92 (2 matches)

STONE, Robert. b. 29-1-1749, Brixton, Surrey; d. June 1820. (Not to be confused with the 'R.Stone' pseudonym used by R.Stevens, above).

    Surrey, England, Hampshire, Kent, East Kent, MCC 1773-74; 1778; 1780; 1790 (10 matches)

STRATHAVON, George Gordon, Lord (5th Earl of Aboyne from 28-12-1794, 9th Marquess of Huntly from 28-5-1836). b. 28-6-1761, Edinburgh, Midlothian, Scotland; d. 17-6-1853, London. Father of Lord Strathavon (Hampshire, Kent, Middlesex, Surrey 1818-42; from 1836 played as Earl of Aboyne). Educated: Eton.

    White Conduit, Surrey 1787-88; 1792 (3 matches)

STREETER, Edward.

    Brighton 1791-92 (2 matches)

SUETER, Thomas. bapt. 17-4-1750, Hambledon, Hampshire; d. 17-2-1827, Emsworth, Hampshire; buried Hambledon, Hampshire. He was a carpenter and builder, also a gamekeeper. Lhb; wk.

    Hampshire, Surrey, West Kent 1772-84; 1786; 1788-90 (67 matches). Single Wicket: 8 matches. First reported playing in 1769.

SWAYNE, Thomas. He was an innkeeper.

    Chertsey 1778 (1 match)

SYLVESTER, –.

    London, Middlesex, MCC, Old Westminsters 1792-93; 1795-98 (14 matches); 1802 (1 match)

TALBOT, Sir George, baronet. (succeeded as 3rd baronet 3-11-1812). b. 14-3-1763; d. 10-6-1850. Educated: Harrow.

    Gentlemen of England, White Conduit, Hampshire, Kent, Surrey 1787-89; 1791 (20 matches). Single Wicket: 1 match.

TALMEGE, – (either Charles or his brother William).

    Middlesex 1790 (1 match)

TANKERVILLE, Charles Bennett, 4th Earl of (succeeded to title 27-10-1767). b. 15-11-1743, St James's Square, Westminster, Middlesex; d. 10-12-1822, Mount Felix, Walton-on-Thames, Surrey; buried Harlington, Hounslow, Middlesex. Educated: Eton 1753-60.

    Surrey, England, Hampshire, West Kent 1773-77; 1779-81 (25 matches)

TANNER, John. b. c1771-72; d. 23-3-1858, Sutton, Surrey; buried Norwood, Surrey.

    England, Select XI 1797; 1800 (4 matches); 1802-1826 (41 matches)

TAYLOR, Thomas. bapt. 18-10-1753, Ropley, Hampshire; death reported on 29-4-1806, New Alresford, Hampshire; buried Old Alresford, Hampshire. He was an innkeeper and gamekeeper. He should not be confused with Thomas Taylor Esq., of Maidstone (Gentlemen of Kent 1785, not 'great' matches).

    East Kent, Hampshire, MCC 1775-84; 1786-95; 1797-98 (102 matches). Single Wicket: 7 matches.

THANET, Sackville Tufton, 9th Earl of (succeeded to title 27-3-1786). b. 30-6-1769, Hothfield House, Kent; d. 24-1-1825 Chalons-en-Champagne, France. Brother of Hon. H.J.Tufton (Kent, Middlesex, Surrey) and Hon. J.Tufton (Kent, Middlesex), son-in-law of Lord J.P.Sackville.
Gentlemen of England, Gentlemen of Kent, MCC 1791; 1794 (5 matches)
THOMPSON, –.
Oldfield 1792-94 (9 matches)
TIMBER, –.
Oldfield 1792-95 (10 matches)
TOWELL, C.
MCC 1791 (1 match)
TOWNSEND, –.
England, Kent, West Kent 1783-84; 1786 (5 matches)
TUFTON, Hon. Henry James (11th Earl of Thanet from 20-4-1832). b. 2-1-1775, Hothfield, Kent; d. 12-6-1849, Marylebone, Middlesex; buried Rainham Church, Kent. Educated: Westminster 1786; Military School, Angers, France. Whig MP for Rochester 1796-1802; Whig MP for Appleby 1826-32. High Sheriff of Westmorland 1832-49, Lord Lieutenant of Kent 1840-46. Prisoner in France 1803-15. Ensign 26th Foot 1790, Lieutenant 1793, Captain 1793. Brother of 9th Earl of Thanet (Gentlemen of England, MCC) and Hon. John Tufton (Middlesex, Kent). Wk.
MCC, Surrey, Middlesex, Kent 1793-98; 1800 (60 matches); 1801 (2 matches)
TUFTON, Hon. John. b. 22-11-1773, Hothfield, Kent; d. 28-5-1799; buried Rainham Church, Kent. Educated: Westminster 1786; Jesus College, Cambridge 1798. MP for Appleby 1796-99. Brother of 9th Earl of Thanet (Gentlemen of England, MCC) and Hon. H.J.Tufton (Surrey, Middlesex, Kent).
MCC, Middlesex, Kent 1793; 1795-98 (48 matches)
TURNBULL, –.
Surrey 1796 (2 matches)
TURNER, Robert.
Middlesex, London, England, Old Etonians 1789; 1791-95; 1797 (21 matches)
TURNER, W.
Gentlemen of England, Middlesex 1789; 1795; 1798-99 (9 matches); 1801-1809 (6 matches)
TWISLETON, Ven. Hon. Thomas James. b. 28-9-1770, Broughton, Oxfordshire; d. 15-10-1824, Colombo, Ceylon. Educated: Westminster 1781-88; St Mary Hall, Oxford 1789-94. Rector of Broadwell cum Addlestrop, Worcestershire, Vicar of Woodford, Northamptonshire 1796-1803; of Blakesley, Northamptonshire 1797-1824; to Ceylon 1802; Archdeacon of Colombo 1815-24. His father was Thomas, Baron Saye and Sele. Twisleton was a distant cousin of the novelist Jane Austen. In 1796, as a clergyman, he was divorced and remarried within three weeks.
MCC 1794; 1796 (4 matches)
TYSON, –. Educated: Eton.
MCC, Old Etonians 1790; 1793 (4 matches)

UPTON, General Hon. Arthur Percy. b. 13-6-1777, Castle Upton, Antrim, Ireland; d. 22-1-1855, Brighton, Sussex. Educated: Westminster 1786. Ensign 2nd Foot Guards 1793, Lieutenant and Captain 1795, Major 13th Foot 1807, Lieut.-Colonel 7th West India Regt. 1807, Captain and Lieut.-Colonel 1st Foot Guards 1807, Colonel 1814; Major-General 1821, Lieut.-General 1837; General 1851. MP for Bury St Edmunds 1818-26. His father was the 1st Lord Templetown.
MCC, Middlesex 1795-98; 1800 (12 matches); 1802-1808 (24 matches)

VALLANCE, John. bapt. 18-9-1759, Patcham, Sussex. Related to P. Vallance (Brighton).
Brighton 1791-92 (5 matches)
VALLANCE, Philip. bapt. 17-5-1761, Patcham, Sussex; d. 13-11-1825, Brighton, Sussex. Related to J. Vallance (Brighton).
Brighton 1791-92 (6 matches)
VECK, Richard Aubery. b. 1756, New Alresford, Hampshire; d. 13-11-1823, Bishops Waltham, Hampshire; buried Old Alresford, Hampshire. He was a hosier and haberdasher. Several documentary sources authenticate the spelling of 'Aubery' rather than 'Aubrey'.
Hampshire, Kent, East Kent 1776-84 (36 matches). Single Wicket: 5 matches.

VENNER, –.
  East Kent 1790 (1 match)
VINCENT, –.
  England, Gentlemen of England, Surrey 1789 (3 matches)

WALKER, Harry. b. c1760, Churt, Surrey; buried 22-7-1805, Brook, near Witley, Surrey. He was a farmer and maltster. Brother of John (Hampshire, Surrey) and Thomas (Hampshire, Surrey). Lhb.
  Hampshire, Surrey, West Kent 1786-1800 (98 matches); 1801-1802 (3 matches). Single Wicket: 3 matches.
WALKER, John. b. 1768, Churt, Surrey; d. 3-9-1835, Thursley, near Godalming, Surrey. His death was the result of a cricket accident. He was a farmer and grocer. Brother of Harry (Hampshire, Surrey) and Thomas (Hampshire, Surrey).
  Surrey, Hampshire 1789; 1791-98; 1800 (44 matches); 1801-1805 (8 matches)
WALKER, Thomas. 'Old Everlasting'. b. 16-11-1762, Churt, Surrey; d. 1-3-1831, Chiddingfold, Surrey. He was a farmer, gamekeeper and grocer. Brother of Harry (Hampshire, Surrey) and John (Hampshire, Surrey). Rhb; occasional roundarm.
  England, Hampshire, Kent, West Kent, MCC, Middlesex, Surrey, Brighton, White Conduit, Select XIs 1786-1800 (130 matches); 1801-1810 (47 matches). Single Wicket: 3 matches.
WALKER, –. (of Aldington, Kent).
  East Kent 1790 (1 match)
WALLER, –. (of Maidstone, Kent).
  Kent 1774 (2 matches)
WALLER, –.
  Surrey 1800 (1 match); 1803 (1 match)
WALPOLE, Robert. b. 1768; d. 18-5-1834, London. Educated: Eton.
  Old Etonians, MCC 1793 (2 matches); 1808 (1 match)
WARD, John. d. c1820.
  England 1800 (3 matches); 1801-06 (11 matches)
WARREN, Charles. b. 19-3-1764; d. 12-8-1829, Sundridge, Kent. Educated: Westminster 1774-81; Jesus College, Cambridge 1780-85. Lincoln's Inn 1781, called to the Bar 1790, KC in 1816, Chief Justice of Chester 1819. MP for Dorchester 1819-26.
  Middlesex 1795; 1800 (2 matches); 1802-26 (21 matches).
WEBB, T.
  Middlesex 1790-92 (4 matches); 1807-1808 (2 matches)
WEBB, –. (of Isle of Thanet, Kent).
  Kent, East Kent, West Kent 1781 (5 matches)
WELCH, Richard. b. 1770; d. 20-4-1809, Swainstone, Neath, Glamorgan, Wales. Educated: Westminster 1779-86; Christ Church College, Oxford 1786-90. Lincoln's Inn 1784. Brother-in-law of George Dehany (MCC).
  MCC, Old Westminsters 1791-93 (7 matches)
WELLER, James. b. c1773; buried 23-3-1847, Petworth, Sussex (from 16-7-1819 he assumed the name of J.W.Ladbroke after inheriting the Ladbroke estates). His father was a clergyman.
  Surrey 1800 (3 matches); 1802 (1 match); as J.W.Ladbroke from 1821-26 played 15 matches (some have been erroneously attributed to the Homerton amateur F.C.Ladbroke in S&B and ACS books)
WELLS, James. bapt. 8-2-1758, Bentley, Hampshire; buried 30-12-1807, Farnham, Surrey. Brother of John (Hampshire, Surrey); uncle of George.
  Hampshire, Kent, Surrey 1783; 1787-89; 1791-94; 1800 (21 matches)
WELLS, John. bapt. 5-1-1760, Bentley, Hampshire; d. 15-12-1835, Wrecclesham, Surrey; buried Farnham, Surrey. He was a baker. Father of George (various teams 1814-21); brother of James (Hampshire, Kent); brother-in-law of W.Beldham (Hampshire, Surrey).
  Brighton, England, Surrey, MCC, Middlesex, West Kent 1787-1800 (102 matches); 1801-1815 (47 matches)
WELLS, W.
  Middlesex 1791; 1797-98; 1800 (5 matches); 1804-1816 (4 matches)

WEST, –.
  Oldfield 1794 (2 matches)
WESTON, J.
  Middlesex 1787 (1 match)
WHEELER, John.
  Kent 1773 (1 match)
WHEELER, J. (of Highgate, Middlesex).
  Middlesex 1794-95 (3 matches)
WHITE, Jacob Thomas. b. c1764; d. 21-11-1831, Brentford, Middlesex. Related to W. (Hornchurch, Kent and Middlesex)
  Middlesex 1791 (1 match)
WHITE, Thomas. 'Daddy'. b. 1741, Reigate, Surrey; d. 28-7-1831, Reigate, Surrey. (not to be confused with 'Shock' White of Brentford)
  England, Surrey, Kent 1772-79 (33 matches). Single Wicket: 1 match.
WHITE, W. Related to J. T. (Middlesex).
  England, Hornchurch, Kent, Middlesex 1787; 1789-92 (10 matches)
WHITE, –. (of Andover, Hampshire).
  Hampshire 1789-90; 1797 (3 matches)
WHITEHEAD, R.
  Middlesex, MCC 1795; 1798-1800 (14 matches)
WILLIAMS, –.
  MCC 1798 (3 matches)
WILSON, –.
  Select XI 1797 (1 match)
WINCHILSEA, George Finch, 9th Earl of (succeeded to title 2-8-1769). b. 4-11-1752, St James's, Westminster, Middlesex; d. 2-8-1826, Park Lane, Mayfair, Westminster, Middlesex. Buried at Ravenstone, Buckinghamshire. Educated: Eton. President of Hambledon Club 1787 and 1789. He fought in the American Revolutionary War 1776-1780, finishing as a Lieut.-Colonel in the 87th Foot.
  East Kent, Hampshire, MCC, Middlesex, Old Etonians, Surrey, White Conduit, Select XIs 1786-1798; 1800 (126 matches); 1801-1804 (2 matches). Single Wicket: 1 match.
WINDSOR, –.
  Select XI 1788 (1 match)
WINTER, Edward. b. 1773, Dartford, Kent; d. 10-3-1830, Dartford, Kent.
  Oldfield, Kent 1794-96 (7 matches); 1806-1815 (5 matches)
WITCHER. –.
  Hampshire 1797 (1 match)
WOMBWELL, Sir George, baronet. (succeeded as 2nd baronet 2-11-1780) b. 14-3-1769; d. 28-10-1846. Educated: Eton; Trinity College, Cambridge 1786-90. High Sheriff of Yorkshire 1809.
  MCC 1792 (1 match)
WOOD, John. (of Pirbright, Surrey). bapt. 1-11-1744, Coulsdon, Surrey; buried 12-3-1793, Coulsdon, Surrey. Erroneously called Thomas Wood in S&B.
  Surrey, England, Hampshire 1772-78; 1780 (23 matches). Single Wicket: 1 match.
WOOD, John. (of Seal, near Sevenoaks, Kent). b. c1745; buried 5-7-1816, Seal, near Sevenoaks, Kent.
  England, Kent, West Kent 1773-76; 1781; 1783 (12 matches). Single Wicket: 1 match.
WOOD, –.
  East Kent 1789-90 (2 matches)
WOODROFFE, –.
  England 1799-1800 (4 matches)
WOOLDRIDGE, –.
  Hampshire 1798 (1 match)
WYATT, Richard Barnard. b. 1762, Hornchurch, Essex; bapt. 28-6-1764, Romford, Essex. Educated: Eton.
  White Conduit, Hornchurch, MCC, Old Etonians 1787; 1789-93; 1797 (20 matches)

YALDEN, William. b. 1740, Ripley, Surrey; bapt. 22-2-1743, Send, Surrey; d. January 1824, Chertsey, Surrey. He was a shoemaker, cordwainer and innkeeper. Wk.
Chertsey, England, Hampshire, Kent, Surrey, East Kent, West Kent 1772-83 (45 matches)

YARMOUTH, Sir Francis Charles Seymour-Conway, Lord. (knighted 1819; from 17-6-1822 3rd Marquess of Hertford). b. 11-3-1777; d. 1-3-1842, Dorchester House, Park Lane, Westminster, Middlesex, site of present-day Dorchester Hotel. Tory MP for Orford 1797-1802; Lisburn 1802-12; Co. Antrim 1812-18; Camelford 1820-22.
MCC 1799 (2 matches)

SECTION 2: THE RECORDS

The following explanatory notes refer to the Cricket Records section.

Match titles
Team nomenclature has followed that used in the ACS book, Great Cricket Matches 1772-1800, which, reflecting eighteenth-century usage, sometimes results in inconsistency. Apparent club sides such as Hornchurch (Essex) and Oldfield (Berkshire) seem also to have organised county matches with no discernible change in their personnel, in a similar way to Nottingham and Nottinghamshire or Sheffield and Yorkshire in the first half of the nineteenth century. Also, the eight matches between East and West Kent sometimes appear under the names of their sponsors, the Duke of Dorset and Sir Horatio Mann.

Ground names
Again, using the ACS book as a guide, place names are shown using their modern form such as Molesey for Moulsey though this leaves another inconsistency as the Moulsey Hurst club play at Molesey Hurst. Nevertheless, it was felt inadvisable to tamper with the title of the club.

Aliases and nicknames
A brief word on aliases and nicknames is also called for. Where known, the player's correct name has been used and this affects two early great cricketers in particular: John Minchin, who usually played as 'Minshall' or 'Minshull'; and Edward Stevens, whose nickname 'Lumpy' is found in almost all the sources. Here, they are J.Minchin and E.Stevens.

Given men
It was a standard practice to use given men so they were common in a large number of these matches, which explains why some players appear for a wide variety of teams. However, it would be too cumbersome to include their details in the match titles. In addition, sources are sometimes confusing in identifying them.

Bowling figures
As bowling analyses were not kept until well into the nineteenth century, the figures are simply of total wickets taken, bearing in mind that until 1836 bowlers were not usually credited with wickets taken from catches, stumpings or lbws. Instead, we have shown average wickets per match, although this is an imperfect tool as we do not know whether players who did not capture any wickets in a particular match were put on to bowl at all during it.

Catches and stumpings
Although specialist wicketkeepers such as T.Sueter and W.Yalden are known, there is no evidence available over whether or not they were behind the stumps throughout a match. On the other hand, it was common for a bowler after finishing his over to stay at that end and keep wicket for the next four balls before taking up his bowling duties again. In view of these facts, it is impossible to separate outfield catches from those taken by the wicketkeeper and this is reflected in the way catching and stumping records are set out. Furthermore, it was not until 1792 that stumpings appear regularly in scoresheets; there were only two recorded in matches up to 1786 while from 1787 to 1791 just 13 can be found.

Winchilsea's XI v Leigh's XI at Stoke Down, 1795 and 1796
When play was suspended in this match in 1795, Leigh's XI were 42/3, chasing a victory target of 78. The game was completed in 1796 at the same venue with the same 22 players when four more wickets fell for 36 runs in registering a three-wicket win. As this match was, for all practical purposes, part of the 1795 schedule, the additional play in 1796 has been included in the statistics and records for the earlier season.

DECISIVE RESULTS
Wins by an innings and 100 runs
Surrey and Sussex beat England by an innings and 249 runs (Lord's)	1793
Hampshire beat England by an innings and 168 runs (Sevenoaks Vine)	1777
Surrey beat England by an innings and 147 runs (Lord's, 2nd match)	1799
MCC beat Gentlemen of Kent by an innings and 113 runs (Lord's)	1791

Wins by 200 runs
MCC beat Middlesex by 274 runs (Lord's, 1st match)	1792
Hampshire beat Surrey by 273 runs (Broad Halfpenny Down)	1775
Hampshire beat Kent by 266 runs (Bourne Paddock)	1787
England beat White Conduit Club by 265 runs (Lord's)	1787
Darnley's XI beat Mann's XI by 242 runs (Dandelion Paddock)	1795
Middlesex beat Oldfield by 233 runs (Lord's)	1795
Surrey beat Hampshire by 221 runs (Molesey Hurst)	1789

CLOSE RESULTS
Tie
Kent (111 & 90) v Hampshire (140 & 61) (Windmill Down)	1783

Wins by six or fewer runs
Winchilsea's XI beat Louch's XI by 3 runs (Lord's)	1793
XIII of England beat Surrey by 3 runs (Lord's)	1794
Darnley's XI beat Winchilsea's XI by 4 runs (Lord's)	1796
White Conduit Club beat Kent by 5 runs (Islington)	1786
Middlesex beat MCC by 5 runs (Lord's, 2nd match)	1792
Oldfield beat MCC by 6 runs (Lord's, 2nd match)	1794

Wins by one wicket
Surrey beat Hampshire (Laleham Burway)	1776
Hampshire beat England (Merrow Down, Guildford)	1777
Hampshire beat Kent (Windmill Down)	1786
England beat Hampshire (Sevenoaks Vine)	1791

MATCHES COMPLETED IN ONE DAY
There is no evidence that any great match 1772-1800 was completed in a single day though we have three for which only one date is given. However, the scores in these prove that play must have extended at least into a second day. These three matches, with run aggregates of 549, 429 and 573 respectively, are:

August 23, 1779 (Broad Halfpenny Down) Hampshire (167 & 182) beat England (112 & 88) by 149 runs.

May 31, 1787 (Lord's) Middlesex (58 & 203) beat Essex (130 & 38) by 93 runs.

August 16, 1790 (Lord's) Middlesex (104 & 182) lost to MCC (145 & 142/8) by 2 wickets.

DRAWN MATCHES
Eighteenth century cricketers showed commendable persistence in giving a match as much time as it needed to come to a definite conclusion, returning day after day following weather interruptions or an intervening Sunday even when the result was a foregone conclusion. In one remarkable instance a match started in 1795 was completed the following season in order to reach an outcome. In this and the other cases it may have been on account of the wagers laid on both the result and individual scores but whatever the reasons there were only two unfinished great matches in the period 1772-1800 as follows:

Hampshire (217 & 63/5) v England (218 & 133) (Windmill Down)	1783
Middlesex (80) v Brighton (64) (Lord's)	1792

TEAM RECORDS

HIGHEST INNINGS TOTALS
453	Surrey and Sussex v England (Lord's)	1793
403	Hampshire v England (Sevenoaks Vine)	1777
355	Hampshire v Surrey (Broad Halfpenny Down)	1775
317	Surrey v England (Lord's, 2nd match)	1799
307	Hampshire v England (Broad Halfpenny Down)	1774
306	MCC v Middlesex (Lord's)	1792

LOWEST INNINGS TOTALS
21	Hampshire and MCC v Brighton (Brighton)	1792
24	Mann's XI v Darnley's XI (Dandelion Paddock)	1795
24	West Kent v East Kent (Coxheath, 2nd match)	1789
25	MCC v Middlesex (Lord's)	1798
27	Hampshire v Kent (Windmill Down)	1789
28	MCC v Middlesex (Lord's, 2nd match)	1795
31	Hampshire v Kent (Sevenoaks Vine)	1775
31	Surrey v England (Lord's)	1800

HIGHEST FOURTH INNINGS TOTALS
All out (defeats)
204	Kent lost to Hampshire by 152 runs (Molesey Hurst)	1776
201	England lost to Surrey and MCC by 15 runs (Lord's)	1795
197	England lost to Surrey by 197 runs (Lord's)	1794
183	Hampshire lost to Kent by 34 runs (Broad Halfpenny Down)	1781

Others (wins)
197/6	Yarmouth's XI v Whitehead's XI (Lord's)	1799
162/8	Hampshire v England (Molesey Hurst)	1779

Note also (wins)
131/1	Brighton v MCC (Lord's)	1792
128/2	Hampshire v Kent (Stoke Down)	1781

HIGHEST MATCH AGGREGATES
In which all 40 wickets fell
794	Kent v White Conduit Club (Bourne Paddock)	1786
772	Hampshire v Kent (Broad Halfpenny Down)	1781
724	MCC v Middlesex (Lord's, 1st match)	1792
713	England v Surrey (Lord's, 2nd match)	1797

Other significant high aggregates
701/35	Surrey v Hampshire (Molesey Hurst)	1789
695/36	Winchilsea's XI v Yarmouth's XI (Lord's)	1799
681/34	MCC v Middlesex (Lord's, 2nd match)	1791

LOWEST MATCH AGGREGATES
In which all 40 wickets fell
208	Hampshire v Kent (Windmill Down)	1789
227	Newman's XI v Leigh's XI (Navestock)	1793
242	Gibbons' XI v Whitehead's XI (Lord's)	1800
255	Middlesex v Kent (Lord's, 1st match)	1796
293	Leigh's XI v Morant's XI (Dartford Brent)	1794
299	Smith's XI v Winchilsea's XI (Perham Down)	1787

Other significant low aggregates (below 240)
144/20	Middlesex v Brighton (Lord's)	1792
174/33	West Kent v East Kent (Coxheath, 2nd match)	1789
177/31	Kent v MCC (Dartford Brent, 1st match)	1793

207/35	Winchilsea's XI v Leigh's XI (Burley-on-the-Hill)	1793
221/30	MCC v Middlesex (Lord's)	1798

RECOVERIES

Kent (104 & 194) beat Hampshire (157 & 31) by 110 runs (Sevenoaks Vine)	1775
England (60 & 207) beat Hampshire (194 & 45) by 28 runs	
(Broad Halfpenny Down, 1st match)	1777
Middlesex (58 & 203) beat Essex (130 & 38) by 93 runs (Lord's)	1787
Hampshire (110 & 138/6) beat Surrey (203 & 44) by 4 wickets (Perham Down)	1788
Brighton (34 & 87/5) beat Middlesex (74 & 45) by 5 wickets (Brighton)	1792
Oldfield (37 & 191) beat MCC (73 & 70) by 85 runs (Bray)	1793
Oldfield (92 & 78) beat MCC (130 & 34) by 6 runs (Lord's, 2nd match)	1794
MCC (80 & 249) beat Middlesex (176 & 59) by 94 runs (Lord's, 1st match)	1795
Middlesex (68 & 85/7) beat MCC (124 & 28) by 3 wickets (Lord's, 2nd match)	1795
Hampshire (171 & 141/6) beat England (226 & 85) by 4 wickets	
(Dartford Heath, 2nd match)	1795
England (126 & 242) beat Surrey (202 & 143) by 23 runs (Lord's, 2nd match)	1797
Surrey (31 & 97/7) beat England (80 & 47) by 3 wickets (Lord's)	1800

THREE OR MORE HALF-CENTURIES IN AN INNINGS

5	Surrey and Sussex v England (Lord's)	1793
	(T.Walker 138, W.Beldham 77, Earl of Winchilsea 56, H.Walker 51, John Wells 51)	
3	Middlesex v MCC (Lord's, 2nd match)	1791
	(G.T.Boult 89, W.Fennex 61, W.Bedster 53)	
3	Surrey v England (Lord's, 2nd match)	1799
	(John Wells 93, W.Beldham 82, T.Walker 53)	

MOST DOUBLE-FIGURE SCORES IN A COMPLETED INNINGS

9	Hampshire v England in 307 (Broad Halfpenny Down)	1774
9	Kent v Hampshire (2nd innings) in 186 (Bourne Paddock) †	1781
9	Hampshire v Kent in 174 (Bourne Paddock)	1787
8	Hampshire v Kent in 225 (Molesey Hurst)	1776
8	Hampshire v England in 403 (Sevenoaks Vine)	1777
8	England v Hampshire in 251 (Merrow Down, Guildford)	1777
8	Hampshire v Kent in 206 (Stoke Down)	1781
8	Kent v Hampshire (1st innings) in 181 (Bourne Paddock) †	1781
8	Middlesex v Essex in 203 (Lord's)	1787
8	Hampshire v Kent in 256 (Coxheath)	1787
8	N-Z v A-M in 154 (Lord's)	1788
8	England v Kent in 206 (Coxheath)	1788
8	Surrey v Hampshire in 285 (Molesey Hurst)	1789
8	England v Hampshire in 275 (Perham Down)	1791
8	Surrey and Sussex v England in 453 (Lord's)	1793
8	MCC v Oldfield in 130 (Lord's, 2nd match)	1794
	† *Same match*	

MOST BATSMEN FAILING TO SCORE IN A COMPLETED INNINGS

8	Mann's XI v Darnley's XI (Dandelion Paddock)	1795
	(J.Drew, A.Freemantle, T.Lord, R.Purchase, J.Small junior, T.Ray,	
	Hon. H.J.Tufton, J.Walker)	
6	MCC v Oldfield (Lord's, 2nd match)	1794
	(C.Anguish, W.Bedster, J.Lambert, T.Lord, Earl of Thanet, Earl of Winchilsea)	

MOST BATSMEN FAILING TO SCORE IN BOTH COMPLETED INNINGS

9	MCC v Kent, 4+5 (Dartford Brent, 1st match)	1793
	(G.Louch, R.N.Newman, John Wells, R.B.Wyatt and Hon.R.Brudenell, Hon.H.W.Fitzroy, G.Louch, Hon.H.J.Tufton, Hon.J.Tufton)	
9	Mann's XI v Darnley's XI, 1+8 (Dandelion Paddock)	1795
	(Hon.H.J.Tufton and J.Drew, A.Freemantle, T.Lord, R.Purchase, J.Small junior, T.Ray, Hon.H.J.Tufton, J.Walker)	
9	Surrey v England, 5+4 (Lord's)	1800
	(J.Tanner, J.Walker, James Wells, John Wells, W.Wells and J.Hampton, J.Tanner, T.Walker, W.Wells)	

NO DOUBLE-FIGURE SCORES IN A COMPLETED INNINGS

Total and highest individual score in parentheses

Hampshire (37; 7, T.Walker) v Kent (Windmill Down)	1787
West Kent (42; 9, S.Amherst) v East Kent (Coxheath, 1st match)	1789
Hampshire (27; 6, J.Small senior) v Kent (Windmill Down)	1789
East Kent (24; 7, John Wells) v West Kent (Coxheath, 2nd match)	1789
England (45; 9, T.Walker) v Hampshire (Sevenoaks Vine)	1791
Hampshire and MCC (21; 6, A.Freemantle) v Brighton (Brighton)	1792
Louch's XI (38; 9, A.Freemantle) v Winchilsea's XI (Lord's)	1793
England (45; 8, R.Purchase) v Surrey & MCC (Lord's)	1795
MCC (28; 7, J.Hammond) v Middlesex (Lord's, 2nd match)	1795
MCC (25; 7, Lord F.Beauclerk) v Middlesex (Lord's)	1798

BYES

These figures include leg-byes, which were not distinguished from byes at this period.

Most byes in an innings

28	Hampshire v England (Artillery Ground)	1777
23	Hornchurch v MCC (Hornchurch)	1789
22	Hampshire v England (Broad Halfpenny Down, 2nd match)	1777
21	England v Hampshire (Bourne Paddock)	1772
20	Gentlemen of England v Old Etonians (Lord's)	1791

Most byes in both innings

41	Hampshire v England (Artillery Ground)	1777
37	England v Hampshire (Bourne Paddock)	1772

Most byes in a match

57	England v Hampshire (Bourne Paddock)	1772
49	Hampshire v England (Artillery Ground)	1777
41	MCC v Middlesex (Lord's, 1st match)	1791
40	Hampshire v Kent (Broad Halfpenny Down)	1781
40	MCC v Middlesex (Lord's, 2nd match)	1791

No byes in a match

Brighton v Hampshire and MCC (Brighton)	1792
MCC v Kent (Lord's)	1793

(30 wickets fell in each of these instances)

One bye in a match (in which all 40 wickets fell)

England v Hampshire (Dartford Heath, 1st match)	1795

Note: Although the score of Hampshire v England (Broad Halfpenny Down), 1772, does not show any byes, this is because these details were not published. Other reports of the margin of victory make it clear that byes were highly likely to have been scored. Therefore, this match is not included in the above list.

Largest innings totals without a bye

226	England v Hampshire (Dartford Heath, 2nd match)	1795
206	England v Kent (Coxheath)	1788
202	Surrey v England (Lord's, 2nd match)	1797
201	England v Surrey and MCC (Lord's)	1795

BATTING RECORDS

INDIVIDUAL SCORES OF 100 AND OVER

167	J.Aylward	Hampshire v England (Sevenoaks Vine)	1777
144	W.Beldham	MCC v Middlesex (Lord's, 1st match, 2nd innings)	1792
138	J.Small senior	Hampshire v Surrey (Broad Halfpenny Down)	1775
138	T.Walker	Surrey and Sussex v England (Lord's)	1793
125	T.Walker	Winchilsea's XI v Lennox's XI (Lord's, 2nd match)	1797
117	T.Taylor	White Conduit Club v Kent (Bourne Paddock)	1786
116	W.White	Middlesex v Gentlemen of England (Lord's)	1789
115*	H.Walker	Surrey v England (Lord's)	1794
107	T.Walker	MCC v Middlesex (Lord's, 1st match, 1st innings)	1792
107	R.Robinson	Hampshire v Kent (Dartford Brent)	1792
106*	W.Beldham	Surrey v England (Dartford Brent)	1793
104	Lord F.Beauclerk	Lennox's XI v Winchilsea's XI (Lord's, 1st match)	1797
102	T.Walker	White Conduit Club v Kent (Bourne Paddock)	1786
		(this century was made in the same innings as T.Taylor's, above)	
102	W.Beldham	Surrey v England (Lord's)	1794
		(this century was made in the same innings as H.Walker's, above)	
102	T.Walker	Leigh's XI v Louch's XI (Lord's)	1794
101	T.Walker	Surrey v England (Lord's, 1st match)	1797

The following 18th century cricketers made centuries after 1800

129*	Lord F.Beauclerk	Hampshire v England (Lord's, 1st match)	1805
102*	Lord F.Beauclerk	England v Surrey (Lord's, 2nd match)	1805
108	J.Hammond	Mellish's XI v Beauclerk's XI (Lord's)	1807
100	Lord F.Beauclerk	MCC v Homerton (Lord's)	1808
114	Lord F.Beauclerk	MCC v England (Lord's, 2nd match)	1809

HUNDRED ON DEBUT

107	R.Robinson	Hampshire v Kent (Dartford Brent)	1792

FIFTY ON DEBUT

78	J.Small senior	Hampshire v England (Broad Halfpenny Down)	1772
		(Small played great matches before 1772 but no full scores are known)	
63	W.Beldham	England v White Conduit Club (Lord's)	1787

FIFTY IN EACH INNINGS OF A MATCH

58 & 56	T.Sueter	Dorset's XI v Mann's XI (Bourne Paddock)	1781
95* & 102	T.Walker	White Conduit Club v Kent (Bourne Paddock)	1786
72 & 102	W.Beldham	Surrey v England (Lord's)	1794
55 & 89	J.Hammond	Middlesex v Oldfield (Lord's)	1795
78 & 71	R.Robinson	Winchilsea's XI v Leigh's XI (Windmill Down)	1795
50 & 82*	T.Walker	Surrey v England (Lord's, 1st match)	1799

HUNDREDS IN TWO CONSECUTIVE INNINGS

125	T.Walker	Winchilsea's XI v Lennox's XI (Lord's, 2nd match)	1797
101		Surrey v England (Lord's, 1st match)	1797

FIFTIES IN THREE CONSECUTIVE INNINGS

50 & 82*	T.Walker	Surrey v England (Lord's, 1st match)	1799
53		Surrey v England (Lord's, 2nd match)	1799

CARRYING BAT THROUGH A COMPLETED INNINGS

33 (50)	J.Minchin	England v Hampshire (Merrow Down, Guildford)	1777
63 (115)	W.Bedster	Surrey v Hampshire (Broad Halfpenny Down)	1778
95 (183)	T.Walker	White Conduit Club v Kent (Bourne Paddock)	1786

93 (1977)	T.Walker	Surrey v Kent (Molesey Hurst)	1788
39 (110)	W.White	Middlesex v MCC (Lord's, 1st match)	1791
106 (171)	W.Beldham	Surrey v England (Dartford Brent)	1793
44 (81)	T.Walker	Surrey v England (Lord's, 3rd match)	1798

Note: The following two instances should almost certainly be added to the above list but surviving scores show the noblemen and gentlemen at the top of the order:

| 53 (90) | T.Walker | Winchilsea's XI v Louch's XI (Lord's) | 1793 |
| 76 (138) | R.Robinson | Surrey v Middlesex (Lord's) | 1796 |

MONOPOLISING THE SCORING

The percentage figure shows the individual score relative to the innings total.

25*	34	73.52%	G.Louch	MCC v Oldfield (Lord's, 2nd match)	1794
29	41	70.77%	T.Walker	MCC v Kent (Dartford Brent, 1st match)	1793
76	114	66.66%	Earl of Winchilsea		
				Old Etonians v MCC (Burley-on-the-Hill)	1791
72*	109/5	66.05%	W.Fennex	England v Surrey (Dandelion Paddock, 2nd match)	1796
33*	50	66.00%	J.Minchin	England v Hampshire (Merrow Down, Guildford)	1777

(he carried his bat through the innings)

65*	102/6	63.72%	W.Beldham	Surrey and Middlesex v England (Montpelier Gardens)	
					1797
94	150	62.66%	W.Beldham	Hampshire v XIII of England (Lord's)	1789
36	58	62.06%	J.Small junior		
				England v Surrey (Lord's, 1st match)	1799

(Small also scored 33 in the first innings of 76=43.42%, giving him a match figure of 51.49%)

| 106* | 171 | 61.98% | W.Beldham | Surrey v England (Dartford Brent) | 1793 |

(he carried his bat through the innings)

MOST FIFTIES AND CENTURIES IN A CAREER

These totals include centuries which are shown in parentheses

W.Beldham	1787-1821	41 (3)	R.A.Veck	1776-1784	5
Lord F.Beauclerk	1791-1825	30 (5)	T.White	1772-1779	5
T.Walker	1786-1810	27 (6)	W.Bedster	1777-1794	4
J.Hammond	1790-1816	22 (1)	John Bennett	1797-1818	4
R.Robinson	1792-1819	22 (1)	G.T.Boult	1786-1795	4
J.Aylward	1773-1797	15 (1)	G.Leer	1772-1782	4
J.Small senior	1772-1798	11 (1)	Earl of Winchilsea	1786-1804	4
W.Fennex	1786-1816	10	R.Clifford	1777-1792	3
H.Walker	1786-1802	9 (1)	A.Freemantle	1788-1810	3
R.Miller	1772-1783	8	T.Lord	1787-1815	3
J.Ring	1782-1796	8	N.Mann	1777-1789	3
J.Small junior	1784-1810	8	R.Purchase	1773-1803	3
T.Sueter	1772-1790	6	T.A.Smith junior	1798-1820	3
John Wells	1787-1815	6	W.Yalden	1772-1783	3
T.Taylor	1775-1798	5 (1)			

The following also scored fifties:
W.Bowra (1775-1792) 2, W.Brazier (1774-1794) 2, J.Finch (1792-1795) 2, Hon.H.W.Fitzroy (1788-1793) 2, T.Ingram (1787-1797) 2, R.Lawrence (1787-1795) 2, Hon.C.Lennox (1786-1802) 2, J.Minchin (17772-1780) 2, R.Nyren (1772-1786) 2, W.Palmer (1772-1776) 2, T.Pattenden (1772-1783) 2, T.Ray (1792-1811) 2, Hon.J.Tufton (1793-1798) 2, Hon.E.Bligh (1789-1813) 1, J.Boorman (1772-1793) 1, T.Brett (1772-1778) 1, W.Bullen (1773-1797) 1, Butler (1789-1801) 1, J.Crawte (1788-1803) 1, Duke of Dorset (1773-1783) 1, E.Hussey (1773-1797) 1, J.L.Kaye (1787-1798) 1, Hon.G.H.Monson (1786-1792) 1, R.N.Newman (1773-1793) 1, B.Remington (1779-1783) 1, R.Stanford (1780-1787) 1, E.Stevens (1772-1789) 1, Hon.H.J.Tufton (1793-1801) 1, P.Vallance (1791-1792) 1, James Wells (1783-1800) 1, W.White (1787-1792) 1 (1).

HIGHEST AVERAGES IN A CAREER
(Qualification: 10 matches or more, average over 17)

		Average	Runs
Lord F.Beauclerk	1791-1825	24.96	5442
R.Robinson	1792-1819	21.99	4311
W.Beldham	1787-1821	21.47	7043
R.Miller	1772-1783	21.00	2058
T.Walker	1786-1810	19.25	6065
J.Aylward	1773-1797	19.24	3869
J.Hammond	1790-1816	18.98	3968
J.Finch	1792-1795	18.68	467
R.A.Veck	1776-1784	17.98	1151
W.White	1787-1792	17.80	267
G.T.Boult	1786-1795	17.66	583

HIGHEST AGGREGATES IN A CAREER
(Qualification: 3,000 runs or more)

		Runs	Matches	Avge
W.Beldham	1787-1821	7043	189	21.47
T.Walker	1786-1810	6065	177	19.25
Lord F.Beauclerk	1791-1825	5442	129	24.96
R.Robinson	1792-1819	4311	111	21.99
J.Hammond	1790-1816	3968	123	18.98
J.Aylward	1773-1797	3869	107	19.24
J.Small junior	1784-1810	3439	144	13.42
J.Small senior	1772-1798	3346	111	16.73
John Wells	1787-1815	3055	149	11.93

PARTNERSHIPS
Falls of wicket were not included in 18th century scoresheets so it is not possible to note records in this section. However, studying the scores, it is clear that large partnerships did take place. The obvious ones are given here.

First wicket

W.Bedster (49) & N.Mann (73)   Hampshire v Kent (Stoke Down)   1781
  Hampshire made 128/2 to win by two wickets and the two not out batsmen scored only 6 runs between them with no byes so Bedster and Mann must have put on more than 100.
H.Walker (66) & T.Walker (55)   Hampshire v Kent (Windmill Down)   1786
  The scores of the Walker brothers total 121 so the odds are that their stand reached about 100.
W.Beldham (63) & J.Small junior (42)   England v White Conduit Club (Lord's)   1787
  At the close of the second day, England were 87/0 (Beldham 52, Small 31) and as they each added 11 runs to their score the next day they must have put on about 100.
T.Walker (138) & Earl of Winchilsea (56) Surrey and Sussex v England (Lord's)   1793
  An annotation on this match in a copy of Britcher's annual reads: 'I saw T.Walker and Lord.Winchilsea went in first and J.Wells went in when Ld.Winchilsea was bowled out.' So the opening stand must have been about 100.
T.Walker (101) & H.Walker (56)   Surrey v England (Lord's)   1797
  The Walker brothers must have put on about 100.
John Wells (93) & T.Walker (53)   Surrey v England (Lord's)   1799
  As Walker was known as a slow scorer, this stand could have been well over 100.

Second wicket

W.Bowra (60*) & P.Vallance (68*)   Brighton v MCC (Lord's)   1792
  Brighton made 131/1 to win by nine wickets with J.Marchant out for one so the next pair added nearly all of the required runs.
T.Walker (102) & H.Walker (70)   Leigh's XI v Louch's XI (Lord's)   1794
  A.Freemantle, the opening partner of T.Walker, was out for four so a stand of well over 100 seems likely.

Third wicket

R.A.Veck (78) & J.Aylward (28)   Hampshire v England (Artillery Ground)   1777
   An annotated copy of the score in the Duke of Dorset's papers says that the pair added 57 for
   this wicket.

Tenth wicket

H.Crosoer (39) & W.Bullen (39*)   Kent v Hampshire (Coxheath)   1787
   When this pair came together Kent needed one run to avoid an innings defeat but they added 79
   and Hampshire struggled to 79/8 for a two-wicket victory.

J.Wood (19*) & E.Stevens (19*)   Surrey v Hampshire (Laleham Burway)   1776
   To the surprise of everyone they hit off the 43 runs needed for a one-wicket success.

Others (unknown which wicket)

J.Aylward (47) & R.A.Veck (16)   Hampshire v England (Broad Halfpenny Dn)   1777
   An annotated copy of the score in the Duke of Dorset's papers says that the pair added 'near 80'
   and they were obviously helped by the 22 byes in the innings.

T.Walker (102) & T.Taylor (117)   White Conduit Club v Kent (Bourne Paddock) 1786
   This pair hit centuries in a total of 296 so they could well have added around 200.

W.Beldham (102) & H.Walker (115*)   Surrey v England (Lord's)   1794
   This pair hit centuries in a total of 259/5 with a next highest score of 12, so they could well have
   added around 200.

BOWLING RECORDS

SEVEN OR MORE WICKETS IN AN INNINGS

8	D.Harris	Hampshire v Kent (Cobham Park)	1792
7	Lamborn	Hampshire v Kent (Stoke Down)	1781
7	R.Clifford	Kent v Hampshire (Bourne Paddock)	1782
7	W.Beldham	A-M v N-Z (Lord's)	1789
7	J.Boorman	Essex v MCC (Lord's)	1789
7	T.Lord	Middlesex v MCC (Lord's)	1793
7	Gates	Oldfield v MCC (Lord's, 3rd match)	1794
7	John Wells	Surrey v Middlesex (Lord's)	1796

TEN OR MORE WICKETS IN A MATCH

12	J.Boorman (5+7)	Essex v MCC (Lord's)	1789
11	D.Harris (8+3)	Hampshire v Kent (Cobham Park)	1792
10	T.Brett (6+4)	Hampshire v Surrey (Laleham Burway)	1775
10	E.Stevens (4+6)	England v Hampshire (Stoke Down)	1780
10	Butcher (5+5)	Essex v Middlesex (Lord's)	1787
10	D.Harris (4+6)	A-M v N-Z (Lord's)	1788
10	D.Harris (4+6)	Hampshire and MCC v England (Lord's)	1790
10	C.Cumberland (5+5)	Gentlemen of England v Old Etonians (Lord's)	1791
10	J.Hammond (5+5)	Brighton v Middlesex (Brighton)	1791
10	C.Cumberland (5+5)	MCC v Oldfield (Bray)	1793
10	D.Harris (5+5)	England v Surrey and MCC (Lord's)	1795
10	John Wells (3+7)	Surrey v Middlesex (Lord's)	1796

FIVE OR MORE WICKETS IN AN INNINGS ON DEBUT

5	Butcher	White Conduit and Moulsey Hurst v Hornchurch (Hornchurch)	
			1787
5	Davy	White Conduit and Moulsey Hurst v Hornchurch	
		(Molesey Hurst)	1787
5	C.Cumberland	Gentlemen of England v Old Etonians (Lord's)	1791
	(he achieved the feat in both innings)		

TEN OR MORE WICKETS IN A MATCH ON DEBUT

10	C.Cumberland (5+5)	Gentlemen of England v Old Etonians (Lord's)	1791

HIGHEST CAREER AVERAGE
(Qualification: average above 3 wickets per match; minimum 30 wickets)

		Average	Matches	Wkts	5inI	10inM
T.Brett	1772-1778	4.33	24	104	4	1
D.Harris	1782-1798	4.21	78	328	10	4
E.Stevens	1772-1789	4.17	73	305	6	1
Lamborn	1777-1781	4.05	22	89	4	–
Timber	1792-1795	3.90	10	39	–	–
T.Boxall	1789-1803	3.56	89	317	10	–
J.Martin	1787-1793	3.30	10	33	–	–
R.Clifford	1777-1792	3.13	71	222	6	–

Note: Fifteen matches in which no details of dismissal have been recorded are omitted from the bowler's total matches in their career record in both the above list and subsequent ones, where appropriate. A further match in 1783 has also been omitted from the total of E.Stevens as he was barred from bowling in it by agreement.

MOST WICKETS IN A CAREER
(Qualification: 150 or more; the average shown is wickets per match)

		Wickets	Matches	Avge	5inI	10inM
John Wells	1787-1815	359	149	2.41	12	1
Lord F.Beauclerk	1791-1825	348	129	2.70	2	–
D.Harris	1782-1798	328	78	4.21	10	4
T.Boxall	1789-1803	317	89	3.56	10	–
E.Stevens	1772-1789	305	73	4.17	6	1
T.Walker	1786-1810	285	177	1.61	4	–
R.Clifford	1777-1792	222	71	3.13	6	–
R.Purchase	1773-1803	220	112	1.96	1	–
W.Beldham	1787-1821	217	189	1.15	4	–
W.Bullen	1773-1797	181	111	1.63	5	–

ALL-ROUND RECORDS

FIFTY OR MORE RUNS AND FIVE OR MORE WICKETS IN INNINGS

54	6	W.Bullen	Kent v Hampshire (Broad Halfpenny Down)	1781
61	5	W.Fennex	Middlesex v MCC (Lord's, 2nd match)	1791
53	6	W.Fennex	MCC v Gentlemen of Kent (Lord's)	1791
50	5+5	J.Hammond	Brighton v Middlesex (Brighton)	1791
90	5	W.Fennex	Middlesex v Brighton (Brighton)	1791
51	5	W.Beldham	MCC v Hampshire and Kent (Lord's)	1794

FIFTY OR MORE RUNS IN AN INNINGS AND SEVEN OR MORE WICKETS IN A MATCH

73	3+4	N.Mann	Hampshire v Kent (Stoke Down)	1781
54	6+1	W.Bullen	Kent v Hampshire (Broad Halfpenny Down)	1781
54	3+4	W.Beldham	Winchilsea's XI v Darnley's XI (Windmill Down)	1790
61	5+2	W.Fennex	Middlesex v MCC (Lord's, 2nd match)	1791
53	6+3	W.Fennex	MCC v Gentlemen of Kent (Lord's)	1791
50	5+5	J.Hammond	Brighton v Middlesex (Brighton)	1791

The following just missed achieving this feat:

49	6+2	T.Lord	Middlesex v MCC (Lord's, 2nd match)	1792

MORE THAN 2000 RUNS AND 100 WICKETS IN A CAREER

		Runs	Average	Wkts	Wkts per match
Lord F.Beauclerk	1791-1825	5442	24.96	348	2.70
W.Beldham	1787-1821	7043	21.47	217	1.15
J.Hammond	1790-1816	3968	18.98	147	1.20

T.Walker	1786-1810	6065	19.25	285	1.61
John Wells	1787-1815	3055	11.93	359	2.41

The following just missed achieving this feat:

W.Fennex	1786-1816	1928	12.85	145	1.65
R.Purchase	1773-1803	1930	10.21	220	1.96

FIELDING RECORDS

MOST CATCHES IN AN INNINGS

6	J.Hammond	England v Surrey (Burley-on-the-Hill)	1793
5	W.Fennex	N-Z v A-M (Bourne Paddock)	1787
5	H.Walker	England v Kent (Penenden Heath)	1795
5	Hon.J.Tufton	Mann's XI v Leigh's XI (Dandelion Paddock, 2nd match)	1795

MOST CATCHES IN A MATCH

7	3+4	W.Beldham	Kent v England (Lord's)	1792
7	4+3	W.Beldham	MCC v Kent (Dartford Brent, 2nd match)	1793
6	4+2	T.Sueter	West Kent v East Kent (Sevenoaks Vine)	1781
6	4+2	T.Taylor	Rest of the Alphabet v A-B-C (Molesey Hurst)	1786
6	1+5	W.Fennex	N-Z v A-M (Bourne Paddock)	1787
6	4+2	G.Louch	England v Kent (Coxheath)	1788
6	3+3	H.Crosoer	East Kent v West Kent (Coxheath, 2nd match)	1789
6	3+3	W.Beldham	England v Hampshire (Burley-on-the-Hill)	1791
6	3+3	T.Taylor	Hampshire v England (Burley-on-the-Hill)	1791
		(the above two instances were achieved in the same match)		
6	4+2	W.Beldham	Winchilsea's XI v Smith's XI (Burley-on-the-Hill)	1792
6	6+0	J.Hammond	England v Surrey (Burley-on-the-Hill)	1793
6	2+4	T.Ray	Surrey v XIII of England (Molesey Hurst, 3rd match)	1795

MOST CATCHES IN A CAREER
(Qualification: 100 or more)

		Matches	Catches
W.Beldham	1787-1821	189	333
John Wells	1787-1815	149	175
J.Hammond	1790-1816	123	163
H.Walker	1786-1802	101	142
T.Taylor	1775-1798	102	139
W.Bullen	1773-1797	113	119
T.Walker	1786-1810	177	116
G.Louch	1773-1797	122	114
Lord F.Beauclerk	1791-1825	129	111
T.Ray	1792-1811	72	102

WICKET-KEEPING RECORDS
As stumpings were so rare at this period, 'most stumpings in an innings' are not listed.

MOST STUMPINGS IN A MATCH

4	J.Hammond	Middlesex v Surrey (Lord's)	1796
3	Hon.E.Bligh	MCC v Middlesex (Lord's, 2nd match)	1792
3	T.Ingram	Essex v Kent (Dartford Brent)	1792
3	J.Hammond	Surrey v England (Dartford Brent)	1793
3	J.Hammond	Leigh's XI v Morant's XI (Bray)	1794
3	Hon.H.J.Tufton	Surrey v England (Dandelion Paddock, 2nd match)	1796
3	Hon.H.J.Tufton	Surrey v England (Lord's, 1st match)	1797
3	J.Hammond	Lennox's XI v Winchilsea's XI (Swaffham)	1797
3	Hon.H.J.Tufton	MCC v Hampshire (Stoke Down)	1797

3	A.Freemantle	England v MCC (Lord's, 1st match)	1797
3	J.Hammond	England v Surrey (Lord's, 1st match)	1798
3	John Wells	Hampshire v MCC (Lord's)	1798
3	G.Leycester	MCC v Hampshire (Lord's)	1798

(the above two instances were achieved in the same match)

MOST CATCHES AND STUMPINGS IN A MATCH

Because players did not always keep wicket consistently throughout a match it is impossible to identify which catches were taken behind the stumps so this list must not be thought of as 'wicket-keeping dismissals'.

8	5ct,3st	T.Ingram	Essex v Kent (Dartford Brent)	1792
6	2ct,4st	J.Hammond	Middlesex v Surrey (Lord's)	1796
6	3ct,4st	J.Hammond	Lennox's XI v Winchilsea's XI (Swaffham)	1797
6	3ct,3st	Hon.H.J.Tufton	MCC v Hampshire (Stoke Down)	1797

MOST STUMPINGS IN A CAREER

		Matches	Stumped
J.Hammond	1790-1816	123	121
W.Beldham	1787-1821	189	49
Hon.H.J.Tufton	1793-1801	62	22
John Wells	1787-1815	149	17
G.Leycester	1790-1808	50	8
A.Freemantle	1788-1810	134	7

MISCELLANEOUS RECORDS

MOST MATCHES IN A CAREER

W.Beldham	1787-1821	189		G.Louch	1773-1797	122
T.Walker	1786-1810	177		R.Purchase	1773-1803	114
John Wells	1787-1815	149		W.Bullen	1773-1797	113
J.Small junior	1784-1810	144		R.Robinson	1792-1819	111
A.Freemantle	1788-1810	134		J.Small senior	1772-1798	111
Lord F.Beauclerk	1791-1825	129		J.Aylward	1773-1797	107
Earl of Winchilsea	1786-1804	128		T.Taylor	1775-1798	102
J.Hammond	1790-1816	123		H.Walker	1786-1802	101

RUN OUTS

MOST RUN OUTS IN AN INNINGS

5	Winchilsea's XI v Leigh's XI (Stoke Down)	1795
	(R.Robinson, T.Walker, F.Reynolds, T.Boxall, T.Taylor)	
5	England v Surrey (Lord's, 2nd match)	1797
	(A.Freemantle, J.Small junior, J.Hammond, T.Ray, J.Lambert)	

MOST RUN OUTS IN BOTH INNINGS

7	Hampshire (4 and 3) v Kent (Windmill Down)	1787
	(T.Taylor, John Wells, J.Small junior, R.Purchase and W.Beldham, John Wells, James Wells)	

UNUSUAL DISMISSALS
Hit the ball twice

	T.Sueter	Hampshire v Kent (Windmill Down)	1786

FAMILIES
Fathers and sons

John Small senior (1772-1798)	John junior (1784-1810)
	Eli (1796)
Richard Nyren (1772-86)	John (1787-1817)
Thomas Assheton Smith senior (1787-94)	Thomas Assheton junior (1798-1820)

Brothers

Robert Ayling (1796)	William (1800-1810)
William Beldham (1787-1821)	John (1794-95)
	George (1800-1805)
Hon. Edward Bligh (1789-1813)	4th Earl of Darnley (1789-96)
William Browning (1791-95)	Thomas (1795)
John Edmeads (1772-79)	William (1775)
John Freemantle (1780-82)	Andrew (1788-1810)
John Hampton (1793-1816)	Harry (1800-1811)
Richard May (1772-80)	Thomas (1772-73)
Richard Miller (1772-83)	Joseph (1774)
Thomas Pattenden (1772-83)	William (1780-86)
Benjamin Remington (1779-83)	Thomas (1780-81)
	Michael (1781-91)
John Ring (1782-96)	George (1796)
Henry Stewart (1788-89)	John (1792-97)
Hon. Henry James Tufton (1793-1801)	Hon. John (1793-98)
	9th Earl of Thanet (1791-94)
Thomas Walker (1786-1810)	Harry (1786-1802)
	John (1789-1806)
James Wells (1783-1800)	John (1787-1815)

Note: Evidence has yet to be found as to whether the following were brothers or cousins:

William Beeston (1790-99)	R. (1790)
	John (1794-1808)
George T.Boult (1786-95)	Abraham (1787)
	Zachariah (1787)
Richard Francis (1773-93)	? (no initials) (1775)
John Vallance (1791-92)	Philip (1791-92)
W.White (1787-92)	Jacob Thomas (1791)

YOUNGEST PLAYERS

	Born († bapt)	Debut
Sixteen		
A.Buller	26/7/1780	19/5/1797
R.Purchase	24/9/1756	4/8/1773
Seventeen		
J.Boorman	18/4/1755†	23/7/1772
S.Lushington	14/1/1782	30/7/1799
R.N.Newman	4/1/1756	21/6/1773
Hon.A.P.Upton	13/6/1777	9/6/1795

J.Beeston made his debut in 'great' matches on 26 May 1794, having been baptised on 17 September 1778. However, the baptismal date cannot be taken as a certain indicator of age since it was not unusual at the time to 'bunch up' the baptisms of siblings of different ages; he is possibly somewhat older than the 15 years 8 months that the baptismal date might imply.

OLDEST PLAYERS

	Born († bapt)	Final match (last day)
Sixty-two		
C.Warren	19/3/1764	8/8/1826

Sixty-one

J.Small senior	19/4/1737	3/8/1798

Fifty-nine

T.Lord	23/11/1755	25/8/1815

Fifty-five

W.Beldham	5/2/1766	24/7/1821
John Wells	5/1/1760†	14/7/1815

The following were approximately **fifty-four**:

R.Robinson	c1765	9/7/1819
E.Stevens	c1735	5/9/1789
J.Tanner	c1772	26/6/1826

LONGEST CAREERS

(Qualification: 28 years or more)

Not all of these players appeared in every season of the years covered.

	First match (first day)	Last match (last day)	Career Years	Months
Lord F.Beauclerk	2/6/1791	12/7/1825	34	1 (+10 days)
W.Beldham	20/6/1787	24/7/1821	34	1 (+4 days)
C.Warren	25/5/1795	8/8/1826	31	2
W.Fennex	2/8/1786	16/8/1816	30	0
R.Purchase	4/8/1773	6/7/1803	29	11
J.Nyren	16/7/1787	20/6/1817	29	11
J.Tanner	12/7/1797	26/6/1826	28	11
T.Lord	31/5/1787	25/8/1815	28	2
John Wells	20/6/1787	14/7/1815	28	0

Note: Though J.Small senior's career from 24/6/1772 to 3/8/1798 covered 26 years and one month, he is known to have played in great matches from the 1760s for which scores have not survived otherwise he would be among the top few in this table.

SEASONAL STATISTICS

LEADING BATSMAN EACH SEASON

The player with the highest average from a reasonable number of innings is shown. Where another player scored the most runs in a season, his record is also given.

Year	Player	M	I	NO	R	HS	Avge
1772	J.Small senior	3	6	0	213	78	35.50
1773	R.Miller	7	11	2	316	73	35.11
	T.White	8	13	3	320	69	32.00
1774	J.Small senior	5	9	1	239	55*	29.87
	R.Miller	5	9	0	242	95	26.88
1775	J.Small senior	4	7	0	213	138	30.42
1776	J.Small senior	7	14	1	423	85	32.53
1777	J.Minchin	4	7	3	149	60*	37.25
	J.Aylward	6	11	0	392	167	35.63
1778	R.A.Veck	3	6	1	121	53*	24.20
	W.Bedster	5	9	1	205	63*	22.87
1779	R.A.Veck	5	9	1	280	79	35.00
1780	W.Yalden	4	8	2	136	52	22.66
	R.Miller	4	8	1	147	50	21.00
1781	J.Aylward	5	10	0	319	73	31.90
1782	W.Bowra	4	8	0	144	50	18.00
1783	T.Taylor	3	5	0	141	66	28.20
	J.Small senior	3	6	0	157	78	26.16
1784	J.Aylward	1	2	1	67	37	67.00
1786	T.Walker	5	10	1	423	102	47.00

1787	G.T.Boult	4	7	2	170	62	34.00
	J.Aylward	6	12	0	296	93	24.66
1788	W.Beldham	10	17	1	381	59	23.81
1789	T.Sueter	4	7	1	155	59	25.83
	W.Beldham	8	15	2	306	94	23.53
1790	J.Small junior	7	12	2	245	51	24.60
	W.Beldham	8	15	0	316	60	21.06
1791	W.Beldham	9	16	1	532	91	35.46
1792	T.Walker	13	23	2	542	107	25.80
1793	W.Beldham	9	16	2	383	106*	27.35
	T.Walker	13	24	3	496	138	23.61
1794	W.Beldham	11	21	1	479	102	23.95
1795	R.Robinson	15	28	1	768	78	28.44
	J.Hammond	18	34	1	800	89	24.24
1796	R.Robinson	4	6	1	250	76*	50.00
1797	J.Hammond	8	16	2	531	83*	37.92
	Lord F.Beauclerk	11	24	2	557	104	25.31
1798	T.Walker	5	10	1	155	44*	17.22
	A.Freemantle	7	13	0	215	46	16.53
1799	T.Walker	4	7	2	283	82*	56.60
1800	T.Walker	5	9	0	168	88	18.66

Note: In 1784 there was only one great match and none at all in 1785.

MORE THAN 500 RUNS IN A SEASON

Year	Player	M	I	NO	R	HS	Avge
1795	J.Hammond	18	34	1	800	89	24.24
1795	R.Robinson	15	28	1	768	78	28.44
1795	T.Walker	16	32	0	662	85	20.68
1797	Lord F.Beauclerk	11	24	2	557	104	25.31
1792	T.Walker	13	23	2	542	107	25.80
1791	W.Beldham	9	16	1	532	91	35.46
1797	J.Hammond	8	16	2	531	83*	37.92
1795	W.Beldham	15	30	1	526	56	18.13
1792	W.Beldham	13	24	0	503	144	20.95

LEADING BOWLER EACH SEASON

The player capturing the most wickets is shown along with his average number of wickets per match. The one with the best season's average is also given if different from the leading wicket-taker.

Year	Player	M	Wkts	Avge	5inI	10inM
1773	E.Stevens	5	18	3.60	–	–
	Duke of Dorset	3	15	5.00	–	–
1774	T.Brett	4	18	4.50	1	–
1775	T.Brett	2	15	7.50	1	1
1776	E.Stevens	6	27	4.50	–	–
1777	T.Brett	5	31	6.16	2	–
1778	Lamborn	5	27	5.40	2	–
1779	Lamborn	5	18	3.60	1	–
	R.Nyren	4	16	4.00	–	–
1780	E.Stevens	4	18	4.50	1	1
1781	Lamborn	6	27	4.50	1	–
	E.Stevens	4	20	5.00	–	–
1782	R.Clifford	4	24	6.00	1	–
1783	W.Bullen	4	17	4.25	–	–
	E.Stevens	3	14	4.66	1	–
1784	W.Bullen	1	8	8.00	1	–

1786	R.Clifford	5	26	5.20	–	–
1787	D.Harris	6	29	4.83	1	–
1788	D.Harris	11	43	3.90	1	1
	E.Stevens	9	36	4.00	1	–
1789	D.Harris	8	38	4.75	1	–
	J.Martin	2	11	5.50	–	–
1790	R.Clifford	10	32	3.20	–	–
	D.Harris	4	24	6.00	1	1
1791	W.Fennex	8	34	4.25	4	–
	T.Boxall	3	17	5.66	1	–
1792	T.Boxall	11	45	4.09	2	–
	D.Harris	7	36	5.14	2	1
1793	T.Boxall	11	43	3.90	3	–
	Timber	2	13	6.50	–	–
1794	T.Walker	10	41	4.10	2	–
	Gates	4	17	4.25	1	–
1795	T.Boxall	15	60	4.00	–	–
	D.Harris	10	53	5.30	2	1
1796	T.Boxall	7	28	4.00	2	–
	John Wells	5	21	4.20	2	1
1797	Lord F.Beauclerk	11	42	3.81	–	–
1798	Lord F.Beauclerk	8	26	3.25	–	–
	D.Harris	3	15	5.00	1	–
1799	John Wells	4	15	3.75	1	–
1800	John Wells	5	25	5.00	1	–

Note: Fifteen matches in which no details of dismissal have been recorded are omitted from the player's total matches per season in the above list. A further match in 1783 has also been omitted from the total of E.Stevens as he was barred from bowling in it by agreement.

MORE THAN 40 WICKETS IN A SEASON

Year	Player	M	Wkts	Avge	5inI	10inM
1795	T.Boxall	15	60	4.00	–	–
1795	D.Harris	10	53	5.30	2	1
1792	T.Boxall	11	45	4.09	2	–
1788	D.Harris	11	43	3.90	1	1
1793	T.Boxall	11	43	3.90	3	–
1795	John Wells	11	43	3.90	2	–
1797	Lord F.Beauclerk	11	42	3.81	–	–
1794	T.Walker	10	41	4.10	2	–
1792	T.Walker	13	41	3.15	–	–

MOST SUCCESSFUL ALL-ROUND SEASONS

(Qualification: Ten matches or more)

Year	Player	M	Runs	Avge	Wkts	Avge
1792	T.Walker	13	542	25.80	41	3.15
1794	T.Walker	11	462	23.10	41	4.10
1795	T.Walker	16	662	20.68	36	2.25
1797	Lord F.Beauclerk	11	557	25.31	42	3.81

LEADING FIELDSMAN (CATCHES) EACH SEASON

Because players did not always keep wicket consistently throughout a match it is impossible to identify which catches were taken behind the stumps. All catches are included in these totals but where a player also made stumpings these are shown along with the man with the best 'catches only' total.

Year	Player	Ct	St
1773	J.Minchin	6	
	R.Simmons	6	
	W.Yalden	6	
1774	J.Small senior	5	
1775	W.Yalden	6	
1776	W.Bullen	10	
	J.Small senior	10	
1777	W.Bullen	9	
	J.Edmeads	9	
	W.Yalden	9	
1778	W.Yalden	9	1
	T.Taylor	7	
1779	W.Yalden	7	
1780	J.Aylward	8	
1781	T.Sueter	11	
1782	W.Bullen	7	
1783	R.Clifford	9	
1784	W.Bowra	3	
1786	T.Taylor	11	
1787	R.Clifford	11	
	T.Taylor	11	
1788	G.Louch	17	
1789	W.Beldham	15	
1790	T.Taylor	15	
1791	W.Beldham	20	
1792	W.Beldham	32	
1793	W.Beldham	28	
1794	W.Beldham	22	
1795	J.Hammond	36	12
	W.Beldham	33	1
	H.Walker	29	
1796	T.Ray	10	
	T.Walker	10	1
1797	T.Ray	17	
1798	Lord F.Beauclerk	9	
1799	John Wells	8	
1800	W.Beldham	11	1
	H.Walker	8	

MOST CATCHES IN A SEASON
(Qualification: 20 or more)

Year	Player	M	Ct	St
1795	J.Hammond	16	36	12
1795	W.Beldham	15	33	1
1792	W.Beldham	13	32	
1795	H.Walker	12	29	
1793	W.Beldham	9	28	
1795	T.Ray	16	28	
1794	W.Beldham	11	22	
1791	W.Beldham	9	20	

COMPLETE STUMPINGS IN EACH SEASON

1778 (1) W.Yalden 1
1782 (1) T.Sueter 1
1787 (2) T.Clark 2
1788 (1) T.Taylor 1
1789 (4) Butcher 1; T.Clark 1; R.Clifford 1; John Wells 1
1790 (2) T.Clark 1; R.Clifford 1
1791 (4) Hon.C.Lennox 2; R.Clifford 1; E.Hussey 1
1792 (15) Hon.E.Bligh 6; T.Ingram 4; J.Hammond 2; S.Amherst 1; W.Fennex 1;
          Hon.G.H.Monson 1
1793 (20) J.Hammond 5; Earl of Winchilsea 4; J.Ring 3; John Wells 3; Hon.H.W.Fitzroy 1;
          T.Ingram 1; E.G.Morant 1; Monk 1; T.Walker 1
1794 (14) J.Hammond 10; John Wells 2; Gates 1; J.Ring 1; Thompson 1
1795 (17) J.Hammond 12; S.Amherst 1; W.Beldham 1; Gates 1; Hon.H.J.Tufton 1;
          John Wells 1
1796 (16) J.Hammond 9; Hon.H.J.Tufton 5; W.Beldham 1; T.Walker 1
1797 (25) Hon.H.J.Tufton 12; J.Hammond 7; A.Freemantle 4; Hon.C.Lennox 1; T.Walker 1
1798 (24) J.Hammond 9; John Wells 7; G.Leycester 3; A.Freemantle 2; Hon.H.J.Tufton 2;
          W.Beldham 1
1799 (6) J.Hammond 3; W.Beldham 2; G.Leycester 1
1800 (7) J.Hammond 2; James Wells 2; W.Beldham 1; T.Walker 1; John Wells 1

Note: No stumpings were recorded in 1773-1777; 1779-1781; 1783; 1784; and 1786.

GROUND RECORDS

Stoke Down, *Alresford*, Hampshire
Number of matches: 12 + post-1800: 1
First match: July 6, 7, 1778, Hampshire v England
Last match: July 26, 27, 28, 1798, Hampshire v MCC
Highest innings total: 257, Kent v Hampshire, 1782
Lowest innings total: 47, Hampshire v MCC, 1798
Highest individual score: 75*, Lord F.Beauclerk, MCC v Hampshire, 1797; 75, J.Aylward, Kent v
    Hampshire, 1782; 75, John Wells, Hampshire v Surrey and Kent, 1794
Most wickets in an innings: 7, Lamborn, Hampshire v Kent, 1781
Most wickets in a match: 10, E.Stevens, England v Hampshire, 1780
Post-1800 match: August 25, 26, 27, 28, 1806, Hampshire v England in which none of the above
    records were beaten

Bourne Paddock, *Bishopsbourne*, Kent
Number of matches: 17
First match: August 19, 20, 1772, England v Hampshire
Last match: September 7, 8, 9, 10, 11, 1790, East Kent v West Kent
Highest innings total: 296, White Conduit Club v Kent, 1786
Lowest innings total: 40, East Kent v West Kent, 1790
Highest individual score: 117, T.Taylor, White Conduit Club v Kent, 1786
Most wickets in an innings: 7, R.Clifford, Kent v Hampshire, 1782
Most wickets in a match: 8, Gibson, Mann's XI v Dorset's XI, 1780; 8, E.Stevens, Dorset's XI v
    Mann's XI, 1781; 8, R.Clifford, Kent v Hampshire, 1782; 8, R.Clifford, Kent v Surrey, 1788

Old Field, *Bray*, Berkshire
Number of matches: 4
First match: August 2, 3, 4, 1792, Oldfield v MCC
Last match: July 7, 8, 1794, Oldfield v Middlesex and MCC
Highest innings total: 155, MCC v Berkshire, 1792
Lowest innings total: 37, Oldfield v MCC, 1793
Highest individual score: 62*, T.Walker, Leigh's XI v Morant's XI, 1794
Most wickets in an innings: 5 (in each innings), C.Cumberland, MCC v Oldfield, 1793
Most wickets in a match: 10, C.Cumberland, MCC v Oldfield, 1793

Prince of Wales Ground, *Brighton*, Sussex
Number of matches: 4
First match: September 19, 20, 21, 22, 1791, Brighton v Middlesex
Last match: September 5, 6, 7, 1792, Brighton v Middlesex
Highest innings total: 197, Middlesex v Brighton, 1791
Lowest innings total: 21, Hampshire and MCC v Brighton, 1792
Highest individual score: 90, W.Fennex, Middlesex v Brighton, 1791
Most wickets in an innings: 5 (in each innings), J.Hammond, Brighton v Middlesex, 1791; 5,
    W.Fennex, Middlesex v Brighton, 1791; 5, J.Hammond, Brighton v Middlesex, 1792
Most wickets in a match: 10, J.Hammond, Brighton v Middlesex, 1791

Burley-on-the-Hill (The Park), Rutland
Number of matches: 6
First match: July 19, 20, 21, 1790, England v Hampshire
Last match: August 7, 8, 9, 10, 1793, Winchilsea's XI v Leigh's XI
Highest innings total: 204, Smith's XI v Winchilsea's XI, 1792
Lowest innings total: 49, Leigh's XI v Winchilsea's XI, 1793
Highest individual score: 76, Earl of Winchilsea, Old Etonians v MCC, 1791
Most wickets in an innings: 5, C.Cumberland, MCC v Old Etonians, 1791
Most wickets in a match: 8, C.Cumberland, MCC v Old Etonians, 1791

Cobham Park, Kent
Number of matches: 1
Only match: August 15, 16, 17, 1792, Kent v Hampshire
Highest innings total: 100, Hampshire v Kent
Lowest innings total: 57, Kent v Hampshire
Highest individual score: 26, R.Purchase, Hampshire v Kent
Most wickets in an innings: 8, D.Harris, Hampshire v Kent
Most wickets in a match: 11, D.Harris, Hampshire v Kent

Coxheath (Star Inn), Kent
Number of matches: 4
First match: August 7, 8, 9, 10, 1787, Kent v Hampshire
Last match: August 4, 5, 1789, East Kent v West Kent (2nd match)
Highest innings total: 256, Hampshire v Kent
Lowest innings total: 24, West Kent v East Kent (2nd match), 1789
Highest individual score: 50, R.Clifford, Kent v Hampshire, 1787
Most wickets in an innings: 6, D.Harris, East Kent v West Kent (1st match), 1789
Most wickets in a match: 7, D.Harris, East Kent v West Kent (1st match), 1789

Dartford Brent, Kent
Number of matches: 8
First match: August 29, 30, 31, 1792, Kent v Essex
Last match: September 16, 17, 18, 19, 1794, XIII of England v Surrey
Highest innings total: 207, Hampshire v Kent, 1792
Lowest innings total: 35, Morant's XI v Leigh's XI, 1794
Highest individual score: 107, R.Robinson, Hampshire v Kent, 1792
Most wickets in an innings: 5, T.Boxall, Kent v MCC (1st match), 1793
Most wickets in a match: 6, T.Boxall, Kent v MCC (1st match), 1793; 6, T.Boxall, Morant's XI v
   Leigh's XI, 1794

Dartford Heath, Kent
Number of matches: 2 + post-1800: 2
First match: August 24, 25, 26, 1795, England v Hampshire
Last match: August 27, 28, 29, 1795, England v Hampshire
Highest innings total: 226, England v Hampshire (2nd match), 1795
Lowest innings total: 74, England v Hampshire (1st match), 1795
Highest individual score: 64, R.Robinson, England v Hampshire (2nd match), 1795
Most wickets in an innings: 3, T.Boxall, England v Hampshire (1st match), 1795; 3, T.Walker,
   Hampshire v England (1st match), 1795; 3, John Wells, England v Hampshire (1st match),
   1795; 3, John Wells, England v Hampshire (2nd match), 1795; 3, R.Purchase, Hampshire v
   (2nd match), 1795
Most wickets in a match: 4, T.Boxall, England v Hampshire (1st match), 1795; 4, John Wells,
   v Hampshire (1st match), 1795; 4, R.Purchase, Hampshire v England (2nd match), 1795; 4,
   John Wells, England v Hampshire (2nd match), 1795
Post-1800 matches: August 5, 6, 1806, Kent v England; August 22, 23, 24, 1809, England v
   Surrey in which the above records were equalled or exceeded as follows:
   Lowest innings total: 39, England v Kent, 1806
   Highest individual score: 64, W.Lambert, Kent v England, 1806
   Most wickets in an innings: 6, T.C.Howard, England v Surrey, 1809
   Most wickets in a match: 8, T.C.Howard, England v Surrey, 1809

Artillery Ground (HAC Ground), Finsbury, London
Number of matches: 2
First match: July 2, 3, 1773, England v Hampshire
Last match: September 15, 16, 17, 1777, England v Hampshire
Highest innings total: 211, Hampshire v England, 1777

Lowest innings total: 117, England v Hampshire, 1777
Highest individual score: 78, R.A.Veck, Hampshire v England, 1777
Most wickets in an innings: 6, E.Stevens, England v Hampshire, 1777
Most wickets in a match: 7, E.Stevens, England v Hampshire, 1777

Merrow Down, *Guildford*, **Surrey**
Number of matches: 3
First match: July 23, 24, 1772, England v Hampshire
Last match: August 18, 19, 20, 1777, England v Hampshire
Highest innings total: 251, England v Hampshire, 1777
Lowest innings total: 50, England v Hampshire, 1777
Highest individual score: 68, W.Yalden, Hampshire v England, 1772
Most wickets in an innings: 5, T.Brett, Hampshire v Surrey, 1774
Most wickets in a match: 9, T.Brett, Hampshire v Surrey, 1774

Broad Halfpenny Down, *Hambledon*, **Hampshire**
Number of matches: 14 + post-1800: 1
First match: June 24, 25, 1772, Hampshire v England
Last match: July 30, 31, August 1, 1781, Hampshire v Kent
Highest innings total: 355, Hampshire v Surrey, 1775
Lowest innings total: 45, Hampshire v England, 1777
Highest individual score: 138, J.Small senior, Hampshire v Surrey, 1775
Most wickets in an innings: 6, W.Bullen, Kent v Hampshire, 1781
Most wickets in a match: 7, E.Stevens, England v Hampshire, 1773; 7, E.Stevens, Kent v
    Hampshire, 1776; 7, E.Stevens, Surrey v Hampshire, 1778; 7, W.Bullen, Kent v Hampshire,
    1781
Post-1800 match: September 10, 11, 12, 1908, Hambledon XII v An England XII in which the
    above records were exceeded as follows:
    Most wickets in an innings: 8, J.A.Newman, Hambledon XII v An England XII
    Most wickets in a match: 13, J.A.Newman, Hambledon XII v An Enland XII

Chidden Holt, *Hambledon*, **Hampshire**
Number of matches: 1
Only match: July 22, 23, 24, 1776, Hampshire v Kent
Highest innings total: 136, Kent v Hampshire
Lowest innings total: 89, Hampshire v Kent
Highest individual score: 36, W.Bowra, Kent v Hampshire
Most wickets in an innings: 4, T.Brett, Hampshire v Kent
Most wickets in a match: 5, T.Brett, Hampshire v Kent; 5, E.Stevens, Kent v Hampshire

Windmill Down, *Hambledon*, **Hampshire**
Number of matches: 12
First match: August 8, 9, 10, 1782, Hampshire v England
Last match: July 20, 21, 22, 1795, Winchilsea's XI v Leigh's XI
Highest innings total: 278, Darnley's XI v Winchilsea's XI, 1790
Lowest innings total: 27, Hampshire v Kent, 1789
Highest individual score: 79, W.Brazier, England v Hampshire, 1783
Most wickets in an innings: 6, T.Boxall, England v Hampshire, 1791
Most wickets in a match: 8, T.Boxall, England v Hampshire, 1791

Langton Park, *Hornchurch*, **Essex**
Number of matches: 6
First match: May 15, 16, 1787, Hornchurch v White Conduit and Moulsey Hurst
Last match: May 30, 31, 1793, Hornchurch v MCC
Highest innings total: 209, MCC v Hornchurch, 1790
Lowest innings total: 35, Essex v Kent, 1792

Highest individual score: 89, Hon. H.W.Fitzroy, MCC v Hornchurch, 1791
Most wickets in an innings: 5, E.Stevens, White Conduit and Moulsey Hurst v Hornchurch
 (1st innings), 1787; 5, Butcher, White Conduit and Moulsey Hurst v Hornchurch (2nd innings),
 1787
Most wickets in a match: 9, E.Stevens, White Conduit and Moulsey Hurst v Hornchurch, 1787

White Conduit Fields, *Islington*, London
Number of matches: 1
Only match: June 22, 23, 24, 1786, White Conduit Club v Kent
Highest innings total: 123, White Conduit Club v Kent
Lowest innings total: 100, Kent v White Conduit Club
Highest individual score: 49, J.Small senior, White Conduit Club v Kent
Most wickets in an innings: 4, E.Stevens, White Conduit Club v Kent
Most wickets in a match: 6, E.Stevens, White Conduit Club v Kent

***Laleham* Burway, Surrey**
Number of matches: 8
First match: June 21, 22, 1773, Surrey v Kent
Last match: August 9, 10, 11, 1779, Surrey v Kent
Highest innings total: 238, Surrey v Hampshire, 1778
Lowest innings total: 38, Hampshire v Surrey, 1773
Highest individual score: 82*, J.Aylward, Hampshire v Surrey, 1776
Most wickets in an innings: 6, T.Brett, Hampshire v Surrey, 1775; 6, Lamborn, Chertsey v
 England, 1778; 6, Lamborn, Surrey v Hampshire, 1778
Most wickets in a match: 10, T.Brett, Hampshire v Surrey, 1775

***Lord's* (first) Cricket Ground (now Dorset Square), Marylebone, London**
Number of matches: 82 + post-1800: 48
First match: May 31, 1787 (play almost certainly took place also on June 1), Middlesex v Essex
Last match: August 28, 29, 30, 1800, XIV of England v XII of Surrey
Highest innings total: 453, Surrey and Sussex v England, 1793
Lowest innings total: 25, MCC v Middlesex, 1798
Highest individual score: 144, W.Beldham, MCC v Middlesex (first match), 1792
Most wickets in an innings: 7, W.Beldham, A-M v N-Z, 1789; 7, J.Boorman, Essex v MCC, 1789;
 7, T.Lord, Middlesex v MCC, 1793; 7, Gates, Oldfield v MCC, 1794; 7, John Wells, Surrey v
 Middlesex, 1796
Most wickets in a match: 12, J.Boorman, Essex v MCC, 1789
Post-1800 matches: there were 48 matches between 1801 and 1810
 First match: June 24, 25, 1801, England v Surrey
 Last match: August 13, 14, 15, 1810, Blagrave's XI v Byng's XI
 The above records were equalled or exceeded as follows:
 Lowest innings total: 6, The Bs v England, 1810
 Most wickets in an innings: 7, Lord F.Beauclerk, MCC v Gentlemen of England, 1804; 7,
  John Wells, Surrey v England, 1809

Perham Down, *Ludgershall*, Wiltshire
Number of matches: 5
First match: July 16, 17, 1787, Smith's XI v Winchilsea's XI
Last match: July 23, 24, 25, 26, 1792, Hampshire v Surrey
Highest innings total: 275, England v Hampshire, 1791
Lowest innings total: 42, Smith's XI v Winchilsea's XI, 1787
Highest individual score: 91, W.Beldham, England v Hampshire, 1791
Most wickets in an innings: 5, Butcher, Smith's XI v Winchilsea's XI, 1787; 5, D.Harris,
 Winchilsea's XI v Smith's XI, 1787; 5, Butcher, Surrey v Hampshire, 1788; 5, T.Boxall, Surrey
 v Hampshire, 1792
Most wickets in a match: 8, D.Harris, Winchilsea's XI v Smith's XI, 1787

Penenden Heath, *Maidstone***, Kent**
Number of matches: 1
Only match: August 31, September 1, 2, 1795, Kent v England
Highest innings total: 130, England v Kent
Lowest innings total: 95, Kent v England
Highest individual score: 53*, J.Hammond, England v Kent
Most wickets in an innings: 3, T.Boxall, Kent v England
Most wickets in a match: 5, T.Boxall, Kent v England

Dandelion Paddock, *Margate***, Kent**
Number of matches: 5
First match: September 7, 8, 9, 10, 1795, Mann's XI v Leigh's XI (1st match)
Last match: August 24, 25, 26, 1796, England v Surrey (2nd match)
Highest innings total: 261, Darnley's XI v Mann's XI, 1795
Lowest innings total: 24, Mann's XI v Darnley's XI, 1795
Highest individual score: 95, J.Small junior, Leigh's XI v Mann's XI (2nd match), 1795
Most wickets in an innings: 4, T.Boxall, Mann's XI v Leigh's XI (1st match), 1795
Most wickets in a match: 7, T.Boxall, Mann's XI v Leigh's XI (1st match), 1795

Molesey **Hurst, Surrey**
Number of matches: 13 + post-1800: 1
First match: June 5, 6, 7, 1776, Hampshire v Kent
Last match: August 21, 22, 23, 1797, England v MCC
Highest innings total: 285, Surrey v Hampshire, 1789
Lowest innings total: 36, Hornchurch v White Conduit and Moulsey Hurst clubs, 1787
Highest individual score: 93*, T.Walker, Surrey v Kent, 1788
Most wickets in an innings: 6, John Wells, Surrey v XIII of England, 1795
Most wickets in a match: 8, Butcher, Surrey v Hampshire, 1788; 8, E.Stevens, Surrey v Kent,
    1788; 8, John Wells, Surrey v XIII of England, 1795
Post-1800 match: July 14, 15, 16, 1806, Surrey v England in which none of the above records
    were beaten.

Navestock **(The Green Man), Essex**
Number of matches: 1
Only match: August 19, 20, 1793, Newman's XI v Leigh's XI
Highest innings total: 93, Newman's XI v Leigh's XI
Lowest innings total: 39, Newman's XI v Leigh's XI
Highest individual score: 24, T.Walker, Newman's XI v Leigh's XI
Most wickets in an innings: 2, D.Harris, Leigh's XI v Newman's XI (first innings); 2, R.Purchase,
    Leigh's XI v Newman's XI (first innings); 2, D.Harris, Leigh's XI v Newman's XI (second
    innings); 2, R.Purchase, Leigh's XI v Newman's XI (second innings)
Most wickets in a match: 4, D.Harris, Leigh's XI v Newman's XI; 4, R.Purchase, Leigh's XI v
    Newman's XI

Sevenoaks **Vine, Kent**
Number of matches: 20 + post-1800: 4
First match: June 28, 29, 1773, England v Hampshire
Last match: July 6, 7, 8, 1791, England v Hampshire
Highest innings total: 403, Hampshire v England, 1777
Lowest innings total: 31, Hampshire v Kent, 1775
Highest individual score: 167, J.Aylward, Hampshire v England, 1777
Most wickets in an innings: 6, W.Bullen, England v Hampshire, 1784; 6, W.Bullen, England v
    Hampshire, 1789; 6, T.Walker, England v Hampshire, 1791
Most wickets in a match: 8, E.Stevens, Kent v Hampshire, 1775; 8, W.Bullen, England v
    Hampshire, 1784

Post-1800 matches: August 20, 21, 22, 1827, Kent v Sussex; August 18, 19, 1828, Kent v Sussex;
  September 25, 26, 1828, Kent v Surrey; August 10, 11, 1829, Kent v Sussex in which the above
  records were equalled or exceeded as follows:
  Lowest innings total 22, Sussex v Kent, 1828
  Most wickets in a match 8, J.Broadbridge, Sussex v Kent, 1827
  Note: the full scores of the 1829 match are unknown

Swaffham Racecourse, Norfolk
Number of matches: 1
Only match: July 20, 21, 1797, Winchilsea's XI v Lennox's XI
Highest innings total: 149, Winchilsea's XI v Lennox's XI
Lowest innings total: 76 by both Winchilsea's XI and Lennox's XI
Highest individual score: 75, W.Beldham, Winchilsea's XI v Lennox's XI
Most wickets in an innings: 3, J.Hammond, Lennox's XI v Winchilsea's XI
Most wickets in a match: 3, J.Hammond, Lennox's XI v Winchilsea's XI; 3, T.Walker,
  Winchilsea's XI v Lennox's XI; 3, John Wells, Winchilsea's XI v Lennox's XI.

Fennex's New Ground, *Uxbridge*, Middlesex
Number of matches: 2
First match: July 23, 24, 25, 1789, England v Kent
Last match: August 19, 20, 1790, Middlesex v MCC
Highest innings total: 150, England v Kent, 1789
Lowest innings total: 53, Kent v England, 1789
Highest individual score: 48, W.Beldham, England v Kent, 1789
Most wickets in an innings: 4, N.Mann, England v Kent, 1789
Most wickets in a match: 6, W.Fennex, Middlesex v MCC, 1790; 6, N.Mann, England v Kent,
  1789

Aram's New Ground, Montpelier Gardens, *Walworth*, London
Number of matches: 1 + post-1800: 1
Only match: July 12, 13, 1797, Surrey and Middlesex v England
Highest innings total: 151, England v Surrey and Middlesex
Lowest innings total: 93, England v Surrey and Middlesex
Highest individual score: 81, J.Hammond, England v Surrey and Middlesex
Most wickets in an innings: 3, T.Walker, Surrey and Middlesex v England; 3, T.Taylor, England v
  Surrey and Middlesex; 3, W.Beldham, Surrey and Middlesex v England
Most wickets in a match: 4, W.Beldham, Surrey and Middlesex v England; 4, T.Taylor, England v
  Surrey and Middlesex
Post-1800 match: September 24, 1803, Beauclerk's XI v Barton's XI in which the above records
  were equalled or exceeded as follows:
  Lowest innings total 69, Barton's XI v Beauclerk's XI
  Most wickets in an innings 4, Lord F.Beauclerk, Beauclerk's XI v Barton's XI
  Most wickets in a match 4, Lord F.Beauclerk

Holt Pound Ground, *Wrecclesham*, Surrey
Number of matches: 1 + post-1800: 2
Only match: August 23, 24, 25, 1791, Surrey v Hampshire
Highest innings total: 112, Surrey v Hampshire
Lowest innings total: 78, Hampshire v Surrey
Highest individual score: 47, J.Small junior, Hampshire v Surrey
Most wickets in an innings: 4, John Wells, Surrey v Hampshire
Most wickets in a match: 6, John Wells, Surrey v Hampshire
Post-1800 matches: July 11, 12, 13, 1808, Surrey v England; July 11, 12, 13, 1809, Surrey v
  England in which the above records were exceeded as follows:
  Highest innings total 185, Surrey v England, 1808
  Lowest innings total 64, England v Surrey, 1809

Highest individual score 86, W.Lambert, Surrey v England, 1808
Most wickets in an innings 5, T.C.Howard, England v Surrey, 1808

A professional cricketer, originally from
Yorkshire, Thomas Lord (1755-1832) was
engaged to create the famous ground that
(albeit after two changes of location) still
bears his name. The site of Lord's first
ground is now partly occupied by Dorset
Square. The creation of such a ground, in a
metropolitan setting, signalised a
fundamental shift from cricket's rural
origins.

SECTION 3: CAREER RECORDS

There follows an alphabetical list of every player that took part in the 237 'great' matches 1772-1800. Particulars are given, in the normal ACS format, of his career dates and playing record in these matches. Where a player also appeared in 'important' matches after 1800, there is a second line giving details for his entire career.

	First	Last	M	I	NO	Runs	HS	Avg	100	50	25	Wkts	Best	5i	10m	ct	st
E.Aburrow	1772	1782	44	81	9	780	49	10.83	-	-	12	3	1	-	-	14	
W.Allen	1787	1793	3	6	2	59	25	14.75	-	-	1					1	
S.Amherst	1783	1795	31	61	7	479	39	8.87	-	-	3					28	2
C.Anguish	1789	1795	32	59	5	367	29	6.79	-	-	3					1	
Annett	1788	1792	6	11	2	80	20	8.88	-	-	-					3	
H.H.Aston	1791	1793	13	23	4	76	15*	4.00	-	-	-					7	
H.Attfield	1773	1788	20	36	4	431	46	13.46	-	-	4					8	
R.Ayling	1796	1796	2	4	1	22	11	7.33	-	-	-					-	
W.Ayling	1800	1800	1	2	1	7	7	7.00	-	-	-					1	
	1800	1810	22	40	6	278	45	8.17	-	-	2					8	
J.Aylward	1773	1797	107	208	7	3869	167	19.24	1	14	49	2	1	-	-	58	
Baker	1777	1777	1	2	1	1	1	1.00	-	-	-					-	
W.Barber	1772	1777	15	29	5	125	26	5.20	-	-	2	12	3	-	-	5	
Barker	1787	1793	4	8	1	60	24	8.57	-	-	-	1	1	-	-	2	
Lord Barrymore																	
	1791	1792	2	3	1	1	1*	0.50	-	-	-					-	
W.Bartholomew																	
	1773	1789	4	6	0	59	30	9.83	-	-	1					1	
W.Barton	1795	1800	17	31	3	327	32	11.67	-	-	3	3	2	-	-	4	
	1795	1817	37	68	4	719	56	11.23	-	1	8	7	2	-	-	9	1
Bates	1789	1789	1	2	0	1	1	0.50	-	-	-					2	
J.Bayley	1773	1783	4	8	0	87	25	10.87	-	-	1					2	
J.Bayton	1776	1777	2	3	0	19	13	6.33	-	-	-					1	
Lord F.Beauclerk																	
	1791	1800	31	59	5	970	104	17.96	1	2	10	102	4	-	-	31	
	1791	1825	129	238	20	5442	129*	24.96	5	25	53	349	7	2	-	111	1
W.Bedster	1777	1794	59	110	10	1335	63*	13.35	-	4	10	26	4	-	-	35	
J.Beeston	1794	1799	7	13	3	76	49	7.60	-	-	1	5	5	1	-	-	
	1794	1808	10	18	5	92	49	7.07	-	-	1	7	5	1	-	2	
R.Beeston	1790	1790	1	2	0	32	21	16.00	-	-	-					-	
W.Beeston	1790	1799	4	7	0	27	8	3.85	-	-	-					-	
G.Beldham	1800	1800	2	4	2	41	31*	20.50	-	-	1					-	
	1800	1805	3	6	2	42	31*	10.50	-	-	1					-	
J.Beldham	1794	1795	3	6	2	21	11	5.25	-	-	-					1	
W.Beldham	1787	1800	117	217	12	4668	144	22.77	3	25	38	170	7	4	-	222	6
	1787	1821	189	348	20	7043	144	21.47	3	38	62	217	7	4	-	333	49
James Bennett	1798	1798	2	4	0	28	17	7.00	-	-	-					-	
	1798	1805	5	9	1	135	73*	16.87	-	1	-	2	2	-	-	2	
John Bennett	1797	1800	10	17	2	142	53*	9.46	-	1	1	1	1	-	-	4	
	1797	1818	61	110	9	1342	72	13.28	-	4	12	53	5	1	-	42	1
Berwick	1779	1780	6	12	4	68	19	8.50	-	-	-	5	3	-	-	3	
Bexley	1794	1794	1	2	1	5	3	5.00	-	-	-					-	
Blake	1773	1773	1	2	1	8	8	8.00	-	-	-					-	
E.Bligh	1789	1798	51	97	5	929	64	10.09	-	1	9	2	1	-	-	22	6
	1789	1813	76	143	15	1311	64	10.24	-	1	12	2	1	-	-	36	6
Bliss	1795	1795	1	2	1	0	0*	0.00	-	-	-					1	
Blunt	1792	1792	1	2	0	0	0	0.00	-	-	-					-	
Boltwood	1778	1778	1	2	0	34	27	17.00	-	-	1					-	
H.Bonham	1778	1778	1	2	0	13	9	6.50	-	-	-					-	
Bonick	1789	1789	1	1	1	2	2*	-	-	-	-	1	1	-	-	-	
F.Booker	1773	1790	45	84	13	835	55*	11.76	-	1	8	7	3	-	-	18	
J.Boorman	1772	1793	55	105	19	810	55	9.41	-	1	5	94	7	2	1	29	
G.Booth	1798	1800	5	9	1	15	5	1.87	-	-	-					4	
	1798	1804	8	14	1	38	11	2.92	-	-	-					4	
A.Boult	1787	1787	1	2	0	3	3	1.50	-	-	-					-	
G.T.Boult	1786	1795	20	36	3	583	89	17.66	-	4	3	1	1	-	-	8	
Z.Boult	1787	1787	1	2	0	18	18	9.00	-	-	-					1	
W.Bowra	1775	1792	50	95	6	1138	60*	12.78	-	2	13	4	2	-	-	40	
T.Boxall	1789	1800	83	150	27	839	41*	6.82	-	-	2	303	6	10	-	42	
	1789	1803	89	160	29	883	41*	6.74	-	-	2	317	6	10	-	47	
Brades	1795	1795	1	2	0	3	3	1.50	-	-	-					2	

	First	Last	M	I	NO	Runs	HS	Avg	100	50	25	Wkts	Best	5i	10m	ct	st
W.Brazier	1774	1794	50	98	7	1216	79	13.36	-	2	15	42	5	1	-	15	
T.Brett	1772	1778	32	57	11	394	69	8.56	-	1	2	104	6	4	1	8	
Briden	1798	1798	1	2	0	5	4	2.50	-	-	-					-	
H.Bridger	1795	1795	1	2	0	7	5	3.50	-	-	-					-	
Brown	1797	1797	1	2	0	1	1	0.50	-	-	-					-	
T.Browning	1795	1795	1	2	0	3	3	1.50	-	-	-					-	
W.Browning	1791	1795	2	4	0	10	5	2.50	-	-	-					-	
R.Brudenell	1790	1793	9	16	2	39	16*	2.78	-	-	-					1	
W.Bullen	1773	1797	113	217	43	1777	54	10.21	-	1	19	181	6	5	-	119	
A.Buller	1797	1797	1	2	0	0	0	0.00	-	-	-					-	
J.Burgess	1794	1795	2	4	1	35	14*	11.66	-	-	-					1	
T.J.Burgoyne	1797	1800	7	12	5	86	30	12.28	-	-	1					2	
	1797	1816	17	30	10	202	47*	10.10	-	-	2	1	1	-	-	4	
Sir P.Burrell	1787	1790	7	14	0	123	27	8.78	-	-	1					7	
Butcher	1787	1793	23	41	9	249	30	7.78	-	-	2	55	5	6	1	8	1
Butler	1789	1797	12	22	0	189	50	8.59	-	1	-					5	
	1789	1801	13	23	0	189	50	8.21	-	1	-					6	
Butterly	1787	1787	1	2	1	5	3	5.00	-	-	-					-	
Z.Button	1793	1798	2	4	0	24	9	6.00	-	-	-					-	
Cantrell	1789	1792	7	12	0	144	44	12.00	-	-	2					6	
T.E.Capel	1790	1790	3	6	2	27	19	6.75	-	-	-	1	1	-	-	2	
Capron	1792	1792	3	4	1	43	21*	14.33	-	-	-					3	
Carpenter	1789	1789	1	2	0	3	2	1.50	-	-	-					-	
Carr	1789	1791	4	8	0	97	39	12.12	-	-	2					1	
Carter	1793	1795	4	8	3	86	34*	17.20	-	-	1					1	
Childs	1772	1774	8	13	0	83	38	6.38	-	-	1					1	
Chitty	1800	1800	1	2	1	0	0*	0.00	-	-	-					1	
J.Church	1789	1795	3	5	2	9	3	3.00	-	-	-					-	
Clair	1797	1797	1	2	0	5	5	2.50	-	-	-	2	2	-	-	-	
	1797	1803	2	3	0	6	5	2.00	-	-	-	4	2	-	-	-	
T.Clark	1787	1791	7	14	1	118	26	9.07	-	-	1					6	4
Clarke	1790	1790	1	2	1	5	5	5.00	-	-	-					-	
Clements	1787	1790	5	9	0	55	17	6.11	-	-	-	5	3	-	-	5	
R.Clifford	1777	1792	71	137	7	1536	66	11.81	-	3	18	222	7	6	-	64	3
B.Clifton	1798	1798	8	15	0	158	36	10.53	-	-	2	4	2	-	-	3	
C.B.Codrington																	
	1797	1797	5	8	2	16	10*	2.66	-	-	-					-	
S.Colchin	1773	1778	10	19	2	150	26	8.82	-	-	2	13	3	-	-	6	
J.Cole	1784	1788	2	4	0	10	4	2.50	-	-	-					-	
Collier	1786	1786	1	2	0	49	35	24.50	-	-	1					-	
Collins	1791	1792	6	11	1	39	11	3.90	-	-	-	13	2	-	-	1	
	1791	1810	9	17	4	56	11	4.30	-	-	-	19	3	-	-	2	
G.Cooper	1797	1800	2	4	2	7	7	3.50	-	-	-					-	
	1797	1807	6	11	3	20	7	2.50	-	-	-					3	
Couchman	1783	1786	2	4	0	15	9	3.75	-	-	-					1	
W.Courtenay	1797	1797	1	2	0	1	1	0.50	-	-	-					-	
T.W.Coventry	1800	1800	1	2	0	4	3	2.00	-	-	-					-	
	1800	1801	2	4	0	13	5	3.25	-	-	-					-	
J.Crawte	1788	1800	56	104	10	877	62	9.32	-	1	10	1	1	-	-	12	
	1788	1803	57	106	10	879	62	9.15	-	1	10	1	1	-	-	12	
H.Crosoer	1786	1790	8	16	1	179	39	11.93	-	-	2					11	
C.Cumberland	1791	1797	23	43	5	332	43	8.73	-	-	4	70	5	5	2	5	
	1791	1804	26	49	6	371	43	8.62	-	-	4	76	5	5	2	5	
Dale	1789	1794	7	13	5	122	24	15.25	-	-	-					-	
	1789	1809	9	16	5	138	24	12.54	-	-	-					-	
Earl of Dalkeith																	
	1797	1797	3	6	0	20	10	3.33	-	-	-					-	
J.Dampier	1786	1787	3	6	0	65	26	10.83	-	-	1					1	
Earl of Darnley																	
	1789	1796	24	45	2	163	21	3.79	-	-	-	18	3	-	-	2	
Davidson	1784	1787	3	5	0	3	2	0.60	-	-	-					2	
J.B.Davis	1773	1773	2	4	1	31	23	10.33	-	-	-					2	
T.Davis	1773	1776	6	10	1	104	40	11.55	-	-	2					-	
Davy	1787	1788	4	7	3	21	16*	5.25	-	-	-	5	5	1	-	2	
Dean	1787	1790	4	7	0	102	23	14.57	-	-	-					2	
J.T.de Burgh	1773	1773	1	2	0	0	0	0.00	-	-	-					-	
G.Dehany	1789	1793	16	28	2	164	30	6.30	-	-	1	1	1	-	-	5	
R.Denn	1787	1793	10	20	6	72	13*	5.14	-	-	-					2	
Duke of Dorset																	
	1773	1783	23	43	1	434	77	10.33	-	1	3	24	4	-	-	6	

	First	Last	M	I	NO	Runs	HS	Avg	100	50	25	Wkts	Best	5i	10m	ct	st
C.Douglas	1797	1798	4	8	0	99	27	12.37	-	-	2	3	2	-	-	2	
Downham	1795	1795	1	1	0	10	10	10.00	-	-	-					1	
J.Drew	1795	1795	2	4	0	2	2	0.50	-	-	-					-	
G.Drummond	1787	1795	7	14	1	36	12	2.76	-	-	-					1	
G.Dupuis	1787	1792	4	7	1	64	28	10.66	-	-	1	6	4	-	-	1	
G.East	1786	1794	12	24	1	196	26	8.52	-	-	1	7	2	-	-	9	
J.Eavers	1800	1800	1	2	1	1	1	1.00	-	-	-					-	
	1800	1802	4	7	2	8	3	1.60	-	-	-						
J.Edmeads	1772	1779	17	33	2	325	47	10.48	-	-	2					12	
W.Edmeads	1775	1775	1	2	0	15	13	7.50	-	-	-					2	
W.Fennex	1786	1800	79	147	12	1838	90	13.61	-	10	10	129	6	4	-	66	1
	1786	1816	88	165	15	1928	90	12.85	-	10	11	145	7	5	-	73	1
R.Fielder	1790	1796	19	36	1	273	35	7.80	-	-	3	1	1	-	-	11	
	1790	1801	20	38	1	281	35	7.59	-	-	3	1	1	-	-	13	
J.Finch	1792	1795	13	26	1	467	59	18.68	-	2	4					15	
Finch	1786	1786	1	2	0	2	2	1.00	-	-	-					-	
J.Fish	1773	1773	1	1	0	14	14	14.00	-	-	-	1	1	-	-	-	
H.W.Fitzroy	1788	1793	41	73	13	757	89	12.61	-	2	7	30	4	-	-	11	1
Flint	1789	1789	1	-	-	-	-	-	-	-	-	1	1	-	-	-	
F.Foster	1789	1789	1	2	1	10	7*	10.00	-	-	-					-	
J.Frame	1772	1774	7	12	0	62	12	5.16	-	-	-	6	3	-	-	1	
R.Francis	1773	1793	47	88	4	866	47	10.30	-	-	7	42	4	-	-	34	
Francis	1775	1775	1	2	0	5	3	2.50	-	-	-					-	
A.Freemantle	1788	1800	89	172	21	1984	58	13.13	-	3	22					38	6
	1788	1810	134	252	29	2807	58	12.58	-	3	31					61	7
J.Freemantle	1780	1782	7	14	5	71	19*	7.88	-	-		9	3	-	-	3	
French	1790	1790	1	2	1	1	1*	1.00	-	-	-					1	
J.Fuggles	1772	1773	4	8	0	51	21	6.37	-	-	-					-	
Gates	1794	1795	7	13	1	77	23	6.41	-	-	-	17	7	1	-	3	2
	1794	1807	8	15	1	89	23	6.35	-	-	-	18	7	1	-	3	2
J.Gibbons	1797	1800	11	20	2	53	17	2.94	-	-	-					2	
	1797	1801	12	22	2	59	17	2.95	-	-						2	
Gibbs	1787	1787	1	1	0	9	9	9.00	-	-	-					-	
Gibson	1780	1780	2	3	0	9	8	3.00	-	-	-	9	5	1	-	-	
S.Gill	1792	1795	11	21	0	130	32	6.19	-	-	1					7	
Gill	1772	1772	1	2	0	7	5	3.50	-	-	-					-	
J.Goldham	1791	1797	22	41	2	273	41	7.00	-	-	2					3	
	1791	1812	26	47	3	305	41	6.93	-	-	2	1	1	-	-	4	
J.Goldsmith	1792	1792	1	2	1	11	8	11.00	-	-	-					-	
Goodhew	1791	1795	3	6	0	27	15	4.50	-	-	-					2	
J.Gouldstone	1789	1793	12	23	1	262	42	11.90	-	-	4	4	3	-	-	4	
N.Graham	1787	1799	51	91	13	581	34	7.44	-	-	5					19	
	1787	1801	53	95	14	590	34	7.28	-	-	5					20	
Grange	1790	1792	8	14	0	124	30	8.85	-	-	2	6	2	-	-	6	
Greenstreet	1788	1788	1	2	0	0	0	0.00	-	-	-					-	
Gregory	1791	1792	5	7	0	28	24	4.00	-	-	-					-	
Grinham	1798	1798	2	4	1	8	5*	2.66	-	-	-	1	1	-	-	1	
Groombridge	1793	1793	2	4	1	36	22	12.00	-	-	-					-	
J.S.Grover	1790	1790	1	2	1	21	18*	21.00	-	-	-	3	3	-	-	-	
W.Gunnell	1797	1797	1	2	0	4	3	2.00	-	-	-					-	
E.Hale	1789	1797	3	6	0	23	9	3.83	-	-	-					2	
W.Hall	1782	1782	1	2	1	6	4	6.00	-	-	-					1	
Hall	1797	1797	1	2	1	11	11*	11.00	-	-	-					-	
J.Hammond	1790	1800	72	132	7	2478	89	19.82	-	17	18	102	6	5	1	115	59
	1790	1816	123	222	13	3968	108	18.98	1	21	37	147	6	6	1	163	121
H.Hampton	1800	1800	1	2	0	5	5	2.50	-	-	-						
	1800	1811	6	11	2	41	15	4.55	-	-	-					1	
J.Hampton	1793	1800	20	35	9	191	34*	7.34	-	-	2	46	4	-	-	10	
	1793	1816	45	78	19	301	34*	5.10	-	-	2	83	6	1	1	20	
W.A.Harbord	1791	1791	3	6	1	15	10	3.00	-	-	-					-	
J.Harding	1792	1800	14	25	3	196	24	8.90	-	-	-					9	
	1792	1810	36	67	4	546	47	8.66	-	-	2					46	
D.Harris	1782	1798	78	135	50	479	44	5.63	-	-	3	328	8	10	4	33	
Hart	1792	1792	1	1	0	26	26	26.00	-	-	-	1				-	
Harvey	1792	1793	4	8	1	39	13	5.57	-	-	-					2	
I.Hatch	1786	1786	1	2	0	7	7	3.50	-	-	-					-	
Hawkins	1786	1787	4	8	0	9	3	1.12	-	-	-					2	
E.Heneage	1796	1796	1	2	1	3	3*	3.00	-	-	-					1	

	First	Last	M	I	NO	Runs	HS	Avg	100	50	25	Wkts	Best	5i	10m	ct	st
Higgs	1789	1790	3	6	1	40	15	8.00	-	-	-					-	
Hockley	1799	1799	4	7	1	19	7	3.16	-	-	-					-	
	1799	1805	6	10	1	25	7	2.77	-	-	-					-	
Hodges	1781	1781	1	2	0	8	7	4.00	-	-	-						
Hogben	1781	1782	6	12	1	98	15	8.90	-	-	-					4	
W.Hogsflesh	1772	1775	11	19	4	63	14	4.20	-	-	-	12	3	-	-	3	
Holness	1781	1781	1	2	0	9	9	4.50	-	-	-						
Hooker	1795	1795	3	6	1	35	15*	7.00	-	-	-					1	
Horsey	1788	1789	2	3	1	1	1	0.50	-	-	-					-	
R.Hosmer	1780	1791	18	35	4	389	43	12.54	-	-	6					8	
Hudson	1792	1792	1	1	0	0	0	0.00	-	-	-					-	
Hunt	1788	1789	4	7	0	60	29	8.57	-	-	1	3	2	-	-	2	
E.Hussey	1773	1797	18	34	2	282	50	8.81	-	1	2	10	3	-	-	8	1
Hyde	1791	1791	1	2	0	14	9	7.00	-	-	-					-	
T.Ingram	1787	1797	21	37	3	404	80	11.88	-	2	2	11	3	-	-	34	5
Irons	1778	1778	1	2	0	4	4	2.00	-	-	-					-	
E.Jones	1793	1793	1	2	0	5	5	2.50	-	-	-					2	
Jones	1787	1787	1	2	0	17	16	8.50	-	-	-					-	
T.Jutten	1791	1792	5	6	0	37	23	6.16	-	-	-	2	2	-	-	3	
J.L.Kaye	1787	1798	8	15	3	141	57	11.75	-	1	-					7	
Kennett	1789	1789	1	1	0	3	3	3.00	-	-	-					-	
Knowles	1797	1797	1	1	0	3	3	3.00	-	-	-					-	
J.Lambert	1794	1797	7	14	4	16	7*	1.60	-	-	-					2	
	1794	1810	9	18	4	34	9	2.42	-	-	-					2	
Lamborn	1777	1781	22	42	9	83	10	2.51	-	-	-	89	7	4	-	1	
J.Lawrell	1800	1800	1	1	0	8	8	8.00	-	-	-					-	
	1800	1810	21	37	4	143	23*	4.33	-	-	-					4	
R.Lawrence	1787	1795	12	23	1	284	69	12.90	-	2	2					3	
G.Leer	1772	1782	44	81	5	1059	79	13.93	-	4	8					10	
J.Leggatte	1789	1789	1	2	0	13	13	6.50	-	-	-					-	
C.Lennox	1786	1800	44	84	4	931	69	11.63	-	2	12	3	2	-	-	32	3
	1786	1802	46	88	4	947	69	11.27	-	2	12	3	2	-	-	33	3
M.Lewis	1773	1773	2	4	1	32	21*	10.66	-	-	-					2	
G.Leycester	1790	1800	19	37	3	400	47	11.76	-	-	1					17	4
	1790	1808	50	94	5	922	49	10.35	-	-	4					32	8
T.Liffen	1791	1792	5	8	0	45	15	5.62	-	-	-	1	1	-	-	2	
J.Littler	1791	1793	8	14	4	28	10	2.80	-	-	-	17	4	-	-	5	
T.Lloyd	1792	1792	1	2	1	10	9	10.00	-	-	-					-	
T.Lord	1787	1799	57	105	15	887	68	9.85	-	3	4	147	7	5	-	17	
	1787	1815	60	109	17	902	68	9.80	-	3	4	148	7	5	-	17	
G.Louch	1773	1797	122	227	14	2010	46	9.43	-	-	25					114	
Luck	1793	1793	3	5	0	4	3	0.80	-	-	-					-	
S.Lushington	1799	1799	3	5	0	17	5	3.40	-	-	-					-	
J.Maddox	1791	1791	1	1	0	0	0	0.00	-	-	-					-	
P.Maitland	1798	1800	8	15	2	66	23*	5.07	-	-	-					1	
	1798	1808	24	47	5	264	28	6.28	-	-	2					2	
Sir H Mann	1773	1773	2	4	0	34	22	8.50	-	-	-					1	
N.Mann	1777	1789	56	103	8	1455	73	15.31	-	3	19	94	4	-	-	21	
Mansfield	1778	1778	1	2	1	17	15*	17.00	-	-	-	1	1	-	-	-	
J.Marchant	1791	1792	5	8	0	81	36	10.12	-	-	1					2	
Marclew	1795	1795	1	2	0	11	9	5.50	-	-	-					-	
H.W.Marten	1797	1800	5	8	1	5	4	0.71	-	-	-					-	
	1797	1813	7	12	3	20	10*	2.22	-	-	-					-	
J.Martin	1787	1793	10	19	5	107	29	7.64	-	-	1	33	4	-	-	-	
T.Martin	1781	1783	2	3	2	2	2	2.00	-	-	-	7	5	1	-	2	
Matthews	1789	1789	1	1	0	0	0	0.00	-	-	-					-	
R.May	1772	1780	13	22	6	112	16*	7.00	-	-	-	11	3	-	-	5	
T.May	1772	1773	5	9	0	96	20	10.66	-	-	-	2	2	-	-	-	
May	1797	1798	4	8	0	90	36	11.25	-	-	1					4	
T.Mellish	1793	1800	22	41	10	187	41*	6.03	-	-	1					2	
	1793	1815	40	78	15	274	41*	4.72	-	-	1					3	
Miles	1793	1793	1	1	0	11	11	11.00	-	-	-					-	
J.Miller	1774	1774	1	2	0	4	3	2.00	-	-	-					-	
J.E.A.R.Miller	1791	1791	1	2	0	9	9	4.50	-	-	-					-	
R.Miller	1772	1783	54	104	6	2058	95	21.00	-	8	29	4	3	-	-	9	
Mills	1778	1781	9	15	0	120	34	8.00	-	-	1					1	

	First	Last	M	I	NO	Runs	HS	Avg	100	50	25	Wkts	Best	5i	10m	ct	st
Lord Milsington																	
	1792	1793	3	6	0	7	3	1.16	-	-	-					-	
J.Minchin	1772	1780	28	49	3	775	75	16.84	-	2	9					15	
Monk	1792	1795	10	19	0	208	32	10.94	-	-	2	18	3	-	-	9	1
G.H.Monson	1786	1792	10	20	1	272	55	14.31	-	1	2					16	1
E.G.Morant	1793	1795	3	6	3	13	6*	4.33	-	-	-					1	1
Muggeridge	1774	1778	4	8	0	19	7	2.37	-	-	-					3	
Mundy	1792	1797	2	4	1	5	4	1.66	-	-	-					-	
Murray	1787	1789	3	6	1	58	33	11.60	-	-	1					-	
J.Neale	1788	1792	3	6	0	68	22	11.33	-	-	-	1	1	-	-	1	
R.N.Newman	1773	1793	19	36	2	189	51	5.55	-	1	1					24	
Nicholson	1788	1788	1	2	0	2	2	1.00	-	-	-					-	
T.V.R.Nicoll	1790	1794	12	21	2	89	17	4.68	-	-	-	2	1	-	-	4	
J.Nyren	1787	1789	4	8	0	40	20	5.00	-	-	-					1	
	1787	1817	16	28	2	199	50*	7.65	-	1	1					8	
R.Nyren	1772	1786	49	90	11	1026	97	12.98	-	2	5	104	5	1	-	24	
Oliver	1787	1787	1	2	2	1	1*	-	-	-	-					-	
D.Onslow	1796	1799	4	7	2	26	6	5.20	-	-	-					1	
	1796	1807	7	12	2	43	8	4.30	-	-	-					1	
W.Oxley	1790	1793	8	16	2	88	11	6.28	-	-	-					4	
Packer	1790	1790	1	2	1	0	0*	0.00	-	-	-					1	
Page	1772	1773	2	4	0	6	3	1.50	-	-	-					1	
W.Palmer	1772	1776	17	31	4	452	68	16.74	-	2	5					1	
Palmer	1789	1789	7	14	2	89	43*	7.41	-	-	1					1	
Park	1795	1795	1	2	1	1	1*	1.00	-	-	-					-	
T.Pattenden	1772	1783	30	56	5	652	72	12.78	-	3	5					2	
W.Pattenden	1780	1786	5	10	1	105	29	11.66	-	-	1					5	
T.Payne	1795	1795	1	2	0	2	2	1.00	-	-	-					-	
Pemmell	1777	1781	3	6	1	33	18*	6.60	-	-	-					3	
C.Phillips	1773	1778	3	6	0	45	20	7.50	-	-	-					1	
J.Pilcher	1787	1796	31	61	2	446	34	7.55	-	-	3	5	3	-	-	14	
A.Pitcairn	1791	1792	9	18	2	152	34	9.50	-	-	1					1	
Polden	1778	1778	1	2	1	10	8	10.00	-	-	-	4	4	-	-	-	
Priest	1792	1792	1	1	0	18	18	18.00	-	-	-					-	
R.Purchase	1773	1800	113	206	18	1930	73	10.26	-	3	16	218	5	1	-	70	
	1773	1803	114	207	18	1930	73	10.21	-	3	16	220	5	1	-	71	
R.Quarme	1792	1793	4	8	0	15	7	1.87	-	-	-	1	1	-	-	2	
T.Quiddington	1774	1776	4	7	2	55	20	11.00	-	-	-					-	
T.Ray	1792	1800	59	109	9	1096	53	10.96	-	2	10	9	3	-	-	88	
	1792	1811	72	134	13	1266	53	10.46	-	2	10	10	3	-	-	102	2
Read	1773	1773	1	1	0	13	13	13.00	-	-	-					-	
C.Redett	1796	1796	1	1	0	0	0	0.00	-	-	-					-	
C.Reed	1800	1800	1	2	0	9	6	4.50	-	-	-	1	1	-	-	1	
	1800	1810	6	11	2	87	51*	9.66	-	1	-	5	2	-	-	9	5
B.Remington	1779	1783	13	25	1	323	62	13.45	-	1	2					2	
M.Remington	1781	1791	7	14	2	133	28	11.08	-	-	1	1	1	-	-	1	
T.Remington	1780	1781	4	8	0	65	25	8.12	-	-	1					1	
F.Reynolds	1795	1796	2	4	1	4	3	1.33	-	-	-					-	
J.Rice	1795	1797	4	7	1	20	12	3.33	-	-	-					-	
T.Ridge	1772	1775	5	10	0	52	24	5.20	-	-	-					2	
G.Ring	1796	1796	2	3	2	7	5*	7.00	-	-	-					2	
J.Ring	1782	1796	89	176	10	2215	82	13.34	-	8	15	1	1	-	-	45	4
R.Robinson	1792	1800	52	99	7	2152	107	23.39	1	10	23	6	1	-	-	14	
	1792	1819	111	212	16	4311	107	21.99	1	21	44	28	3	-	-	25	
Rubegall	1794	1794	1	2	1	5	3*	5.00	-	-	-	1	1	-	-	-	
C.Russell	1795	1795	1	2	1	8	8*	8.00	-	-	-					-	
J.Russell	1787	1793	6	12	1	52	12	4.72	-	-	-					5	
Sadler	1793	1793	1	2	1	0	0*	0.00	-	-	-					-	
Sale	1791	1793	4	8	1	20	6	2.85	-	-	-					1	
T.Saunderson	1797	1797	1	2	0	2	1	1.00	-	-	-					-	
T.Scott	1789	1798	29	55	1	602	44*	11.14	-	-	7					36	
Scott	1793	1797	3	6	1	30	9	6.00	-	-	-					-	
T.Selby	1790	1790	1	2	0	20	10	10.00	-	-	-					1	
T.Shackle	1789	1796	26	50	3	486	37	10.34	-	-	3	1	1	-	-	10	
	1789	1809	29	56	4	590	40	11.34	-	-	5	1	1	-	-	10	
D.Sharpe	1792	1792	1	1	0	9	9	9.00	-	-	-					1	

	First	Last	M	I	NO	Runs	HS	Avg	100	50	25	Wkts	Best	5i	10m	ct	st
J.Shelley	1792	1795	8	15	0	98	31	6.53	-	-	1					1	
G.Shepheard	1796	1796	1	1	0	1	1	1.00	-	-	-					-	
R.Simmons	1772	1779	13	22	1	133	27	6.33	-	-	1					11	
Simmons	1790	1791	3	6	0	65	26	10.83	-	-	1					3	
T.Skinner	1781	1781	1	2	1	3	3*	3.00	-	-	-					-	
C.Slater	1787	1787	3	5	0	48	23	9.60	-	-	-					2	
E.Small	1796	1796	1	2	1	0	0*	0.00	-	-	-					-	
J.Small senior	1772	1798	111	209	9	3346	138	16.73	1	10	34	4	3	-	-	76	
J.Small junior	1784	1800	104	195	9	2695	95	14.48	-	8	29					53	
	1784	1810	144	269	13	3439	95	13.43	-	8	35					75	
Small	1788	1788	1	2	0	2	1	1.00	-	-	-					2	
J.Smith	1792	1800	7	13	1	84	30	7.00	-	-	1					4	
T.A.Smith senior																	
	1787	1794	43	79	6	461	30*	6.31	-	-	2	3	2	-		17	
T.A.Smith junior																	
	1798	1798	3	6	0	64	25	10.66	-	-	1					1	
	1798	1820	40	76	8	1061	86	15.60	-	3	10	5	2	-	-	26	1
Soane	1795	1795	2	4	0	22	11	5.50	-	-	-					-	
Spencer	1793	1793	1	2	0	2	2	1.00	-	-	-					-	
R.Stanford	1780	1787	8	15	1	171	73	12.21	-	1	-					5	
Stanhope	1787	1798	6	10	0	35	11	3.50	-	-	-	1	1	-	-	-	
E.Stevens	1772	1789	83	147	39	822	52	7.61	-	1	2	305	6	6	1	45	
J.Stevens	1789	1793	11	22	2	176	45	8.80	-	-	1					5	
R.Stevens	1797	1799	3	5	0	17	7	3.40	-	-	-					-	
H.Stewart	1788	1789	2	4	0	9	4	2.25	-	-	-					-	
	1788	1806	3	6	2	13	4	3.25	-	-	-					-	
J.Stewart	1792	1797	2	3	0	10	4	3.33	-	-	-					1	
P.Stewart	1772	1779	16	28	5	196	15*	8.52	-	-	-	0		-	-	4	
R.Stewart	1791	1792	2	4	1	23	17	7.66	-	-	-					-	
R.Stone	1773	1790	10	18	1	117	35	6.88	-	-	1					3	
Lord Strathavon																	
	1787	1792	3	5	3	33	17	16.50	-	-	-					-	
E.Streeter	1791	1792	2	3	0	4	3	1.33	-	-	-	3	2	-	-	-	
T.Sueter	1772	1790	67	124	7	1969	67	16.82	-	6	18					47	1
T.Swayne	1778	1778	1	1	0	5	5	5.00	-	-	-					-	
Sylvester	1792	1798	14	24	10	103	17*	7.35	-	-	-	16	4	-	-	6	
	1792	1802	15	25	10	109	17*	7.26	-	-	-	17	4	-	-	6	
G.Talbot	1787	1791	20	39	7	192	28	6.00	-	-	1					4	
Talmege	1790	1790	1	2	0	11	8	5.50	-	-	-					-	
Earl of Tankerville																	
	1773	1781	25	48	0	515	46	10.72	-	-	5					18	
J.Tanner	1797	1800	4	8	3	21	8	4.20	-	-	-	1	1	-	-	-	
	1797	1826	45	81	14	413	34	6.16	-	-	2	42	5	1	-	28	1
T.Taylor	1775	1798	102	189	12	1817	117	10.26	1	4	12	90	5	2	-	139	1
Earl of Thanet	1791	1794	5	10	0	48	17	4.80	-	-	-					1	
Thompson	1792	1794	9	18	2	112	18	7.00	-	-	-	14	2	-	-	3	1
Timber	1792	1795	10	19	6	91	15	7.00	-	-	-	39	4	-	-	6	
C.Towell	1791	1791	1	1	0	2	2	2.00	-	-	-					-	
Townsend	1783	1786	5	9	0	107	22	11.88	-	-	-					-	
H.J.Tufton	1793	1800	60	115	11	888	71	8.53	-	2	4					45	20
	1793	1801	62	119	13	900	71	8.49	-	2	4					46	23
J.Tufton	1793	1798	48	94	9	1049	61	12.34	-	2	13	14	4	-	-	31	
Turnbull	1796	1796	2	3	1	1	1	0.50	-	-	-					-	
R.Turner	1789	1797	21	38	6	214	17	6.68	-	-	-	31	5	2	-	8	
W.Turner	1789	1799	9	15	3	49	12	4.08	-	-	-	3	2	-	-	1	
	1789	1809	15	24	6	78	19	4.33	-	-	-	4	2	-	-	1	
T.J.Twisleton	1794	1796	4	7	0	24	11	3.42	-	-	-					1	
Tyson	1790	1793	4	7	1	29	14	4.83	-	-	-					4	
A.P.Upton	1795	1800	12	22	5	130	30*	7.64	-	-	1					6	
	1795	1808	36	64	11	556	44*	10.49	-	-	6	1	1	-	-	25	
J.Vallance	1791	1792	5	8	4	59	17	14.75	-	-	-					3	
P.Vallance	1791	1792	6	10	1	153	68*	17.00	-	1	1					3	
R.A.Veck	1776	1784	36	68	4	1151	79	17.98	-	5	9	3	1	-	-	22	
Venner	1790	1790	1	2	1	0	0*	0.00	-	-	-					1	
Vincent	1789	1789	3	5	0	50	29	10.00	-	-	1					1	
H.Walker	1786	1800	98	180	4	2658	115*	15.10	1	8	26					137	
	1786	1802	101	186	4	2677	115*	14.70	1	8	26					142	

	First	Last	M	I	NO	Runs	HS	Avg	100	50	25	Wkts	Best	5i	10m	ct	st
J.Walker	1789	1800	44	85	5	589	35	7.36	-	-	6					17	
	1789	1806	52	101	6	704	35	7.41	-	-	6					24	
T.Walker	1786	1800	130	244	15	4932	138	21.53	6	20	41	240	6	4	-	91	4
	1786	1810	177	335	20	6065	138	19.25	6	21	55	284	6	4	-	116	6
Walker	1790	1790	1	2	1	0	0*	0.00	-	-	-	1	1	-	-	-	
Waller	1774	1774	2	2	0	8	6	4.00	-	-	-					3	
Waller	1800	1800	1	2	1	11	6*	11.00	-	-	-					2	
	1800	1803	2	4	2	18	7	9.00	-	-	-					2	
R.Walpole	1793	1793	2	4	0	19	14	4.75	-	-	-					2	
	1793	1808	3	6	0	20	14	3.33	-	-	-					2	
J.Ward	1800	1800	3	3	0	20	9	6.66	-	-	-	9	4	-	-	4	
	1800	1806	14	24	4	180	36	9.00	-	-	2	23	4	-	-	8	
C.Warren	1795	1800	2	4	0	1	1	0.25	-	-	-					1	
	1795	1826	23	41	4	222	6	6.00	-	-	1	3	1	-	-	6	
T.Webb	1790	1792	4	6	0	52	35	8.66	-	-	1					6	
	1790	1808	6	10	0	78	35	7.80	-	-	1					7	
Webb	1781	1781	5	9	0	36	17	4.00	-	-	-					1	
R.Welch	1791	1793	7	13	1	54	12*	4.50	-	-	-					1	
J.Weller	1800	1800	3	4	1	15	10	5.00	-	-	-					1	
	1800	1826	19	30	7	73	12*	3.17	-	-	-	1	1	-	-	1	
James Wells	1783	1800	21	38	5	260	80	7.87	-	1	1					5	2
John Wells	1787	1800	102	186	10	2418	93	13.73	-	6	24	198	7	9	1	140	15
	1787	1815	149	275	19	3055	93	11.93	-	6	29	359	7	12	1	175	17
W.Wells	1791	1800	5	9	1	51	13	6.37	-	-	-						
	1791	1816	9	16	1	103	19	6.86	-	-	-					1	
West	1794	1794	2	4	1	19	9	6.33	-	-	-					2	
J.Weston	1787	1787	1	1	1	17	17*	-	-	-	-	4	3	-	-	1	
J.Wheeler	1773	1773	1	2	0	1	1	0.50	-	-	-	0	-	-	-	-	
J.Wheeler	1794	1795	3	6	0	26	11	4.33	-	-	-					2	
J.T.White	1791	1791	1	2	0	13	11	6.50	-	-	-					1	
T.White	1772	1779	33	62	4	907	69	15.63	-	5	7	23	4	-	-	15	
W.White	1787	1792	10	17	2	267	116	17.80	1	-	1	3	2	-	-	2	
White	1789	1797	3	6	1	17	6	3.40	-	-	-					1	
R.Whitehead	1795	1800	14	27	2	201	32	8.04	-	-	4					6	
Williams	1798	1798	3	6	0	14	10	2.33	-	-	-					1	
Wilson	1797	1797	1	2	1	0	0*	0.00	-	-	-					-	
Earl of Winchilsea																	
	1786	1800	126	240	9	2057	76	8.90	-	4	12	4	2	-	-	45	4
	1786	1804	128	243	10	2064	76	8.85	-	4	12	4	2	-	-	45	4
Windsor	1788	1788	1	2	0	1	1	0.50	-	-	-					-	
E.Winter	1794	1796	7	14	3	122	34	11.09	-	-	1					-	
	1794	1815	12	24	5	166	34	8.73	-	-	2					3	
Witcher	1797	1797	1	2	0	3	2	1.50	-	-	-					-	
G.Wombwell	1792	1792	1	2	1	19	19	19.00	-	-	-					-	
J.Wood (Surrey)																	
	1772	1780	23	41	6	303	26	8.65	-	-	1	45	5	1	-	17	
J.Wood (Kent)	1773	1783	12	20	4	150	37	9.37	-	-	2	6	3	-	-	9	
Wood	1789	1790	2	4	0	17	11	4.25	-	-	-					1	
Woodroffe	1799	1800	4	7	2	5	5	1.00	-	-	-					-	
Wooldridge	1798	1798	1	2	0	11	7	5.50	-	-	-					-	
R.B.Wyatt	1787	1797	20	38	3	312	39	8.91	-	-	4	5	2	-	-	26	
W.Yalden	1772	1783	45	86	11	1151	88	15.34	-	3	11					64	1
Lord Yarmouth																	
	1799	1799	2	3	1	4	2*	2.00	-	-	-					-	

SECTION 4: *GREAT CRICKET MATCHES 1772-1800*
ERRATA AND ADDENDA

This section is closely based on an article by Keith Warsop in the *Cricket Statistician* no. 160 (Winter 2012).

In his preface to the 2010 ACS publication *Great Cricket Matches 1772-1800*, editor John Bryant wrote: "We acknowledge that a book such as this can never represent the last word on its subject. Errors will always creep in despite all efforts to exclude them. More fundamentally, research is continuing and will undoubtedly uncover new information that questions, or contradicts, the version of events that is presented here."

Research has indeed continued and new information has consequently been uncovered, principally by Ian Maun and Martin Wilson, while Keith Warsop has acted as a 'clearing house' for their finds, as well as noting John Bryant's view that "errors will always creep in" and therefore combing the ACS book to try to correct them.

Page 21. Other excluded matches

Regarding the MCC v WCC match in 1788, new research has more clearly identified MCC's opponents. *The World* of June 27 announces a match between "eleven Noblemen and Gentlemen of the Marybone (sic) Club and eleven Gentlemen of Friday's White Conduit Club" A similar, previously unknown, match on August 13 and 14 was reported in the *General Advertiser* for August 16: "The following is a short state of the game of Cricket, that was played on Wednesday and Thursday last, by the Mary-le-bone Club against the Wednesday's White-conduit Club. Mary-le-bone: First innings 134; Second ditto 58/Total 192. White-conduit: First innings 126; Second ditto 47/Total 173. Majority for Mary-le-bone 19. The return match is to be on Tuesday next [August 19] at the same place." A report of the return match, if played, has not yet been found. From these reports it seems that different clubs were based on certain days of the week at White Conduit Fields.

Pages 27-31. Continuity and change: cricket then and now

On page 28, the fifth paragraph down states: "Teams arriving to play a match would not find themselves presented with the close-mown, lovingly-prepared batting strip that we expect today. Instead, the visiting captain would choose to have stumps pitched anywhere within 30 yards of a point stipulated by the home team, so the pitch would be no different from any other part of the playing area".

It should be made clear that this comment applies specifically to the pitch, i.e. the 22 yards between the wickets. It was not intended to imply that ground preparation, in a wider sense, was non-existent. While it obviously did not come anywhere near the standard reached in more modern times, there is in fact evidence that such preparation did take place.

During 1787, the first season for Thomas Lord's new ground in Marylebone, the *London Chronicle* of June 21, reporting on the first day's play in the match between the White Conduit Club and England, says: "Upwards of 2,000 persons were within the ground, who conducted themselves with the utmost decorum; the utility of the batten fence was evident, as it kept out all improper spectators. The ground, though somewhat rough at present, will be laid out next year like a bowling green."

The revised Laws of 1788 include the following new item: "It shall not be lawful for either party during a match, without the consent of the other, to alter the ground, by rolling, watering, covering, mowing, or beating. This rule is not meant to prevent a striker from beating the ground with his bat near where he stands, during the innings, or to prevent the bowler from filling up holes, watering his ground, or using sawdust, etc, when the ground is wet." Presumably, rolling, watering and so on took place before a match and, as mentioned in the new Law, could also be carried out during it if consent was obtained from the opposition. In any case, such a Law would not have become necessary unless ground preparation was already in use and needed to be regulated.

But note that these contemporary sources refer to the ground, not the pitch; there is nothing in them to imply that the actual pitch was prepared with a special dedication in the way it is today. Indeed, this could not have been the case because the laws provided that the wickets might be pitched anywhere within thirty yards of a point chosen either by the winners of the toss (until 1774) or by the visiting team (from 1774).

Martin Wilson has found a 1727 poem that mentions the preparation of ground, although in the context of a bowling green. Still, this establishes the fact that the techniques were around at the time:
"Like Time, the Swain / Whets his unrighteous Scythe; and shaves the Plain. / ... The heavy Roller next he tugs along, ... / And every rising Prominence subdues."
Note the mention of that well-known cricketing implement, the heavy roller.

Papge 33-270. The Matches 1772-1800

Since Great Cricket Matches 1772-1800 was compiled, a new source has been identified that provides apparently genuine contemporary or near-contemporary printed material covering the period 1786-1790. It includes versions of a number of 'great' matches that differ from other sources such as Epps and Bentley, as well as new versions of other matches including three that appear to be previously unknown (although the sides are not strong enough for these matches to qualify as 'great'). This new material has informed many of the corrections below; these instances are marked with an asterisk.

The material is in a private collection and the owner has stipulated that no details may be given that might indicate where it is located or by whom it is owned. In the circumstances, it is not possible to provide any further information.

Page
34   This is the first full score of a great match to appear in a newspaper. It was published in the Reading Mercury of 29 June 1772, whence where it was transcribed by Waghorn. However, the Reading Mercury score does not gives byes or innings totals, only the individual batsmen's scores. The innings totals were added by Waghorn after totalling up the individual details from the Reading Mercury. Other newspapers report on the match but without giving a scoresheet.

67   HC 6/7 has better batting orders. England: Wood, White, Booker, Minchin, Miller, Bullen, Bowra, Yalden, Clifford, Stevens, Lamborn. Hampshire: Veck, Bedster, Small sen., Leer, Taylor, Sueter, Mann, Francis, Nyren, Aburrow, Brett.

72   For B.Rimmington read B.Remington and in all subsequent games.

78   For T.Rimmington read T.Remington and in all subsequent games.

81   For M.Rimmington read M.Remington and in all subsequent games.

87   In the footnotes, read 'implies a score of 109-6 at that point', instead of '190-6'.

94   John Wells was baptised on 5 January 1760, thus not born in 1768 as suggested in the footnote. This raises the possibility that 'J.Wells' appearing in this match may have been John rather than James, but there is no definite evidence either way.

99   Another version has A to C (2) all out 82 with adjustments to individual scores but all other sources agree on 92.*

101   Our only source for this match was the one in SB but now a contemporary printed score has been found. This appears to be the one used by Haygarth for inclusion in SB as it matches the score there in every detail, extending to the omission of the venue.*

102   Our only source for this match was the one in SB but now a contemporary printed score has been found. This appears to be the one used by Haygarth for inclusion in SB as it matches the score there in every detail.*

109	Another source has slightly better batting orders, which suggests that the version in the book is in dismissal order. The new orders are: A to M: Brazier, Bedster, Bullen, Beldham, Taylor, Clifford, Booker, Mann, Louch, Lord, Harris. N to Z: T.Walker, H.Walker, Small sen., Ring, Fennex, Aylward, Small jun., John Wells, Purchase, James Wells, Stevens.*
110	Another version of the score shows Nyren as Nyland, substantiating the identification of Nyland as Nyren in the score on page 131.*
121	Another version in Hampshire (2) shows Purchase b Stevens 0, which would mean Hampshire won by three wickets, though this source does not record the result. As this version offers a more contemporary source than Epps, the oldest we had access to, this should perhaps be accepted as an authentic correction. However, it is not that simple. Small sen. was also b Stevens 0, so it is possible that the compiler of this particular score suffered a simple case of 'eye slippage' while looking at his original copy.*
127	Some contemporary sources give the match title as Amherst v Mann.
131	See note above to match on page 110 re identification of Nyland as Nyren.
132	Another contemporary version also includes Kennett rather than Venner who erroneously appears in the SB score.*
135	Another source has better batting orders. Hampshire: Freemantle, Scott, Small sen., Purchase, Small jun., Mann, Taylor, Winchilsea, Stewart, Louch, Harris. Kent: Pilcher, Clifford, Aylward, Brazier, Ring, Crawte, Crosoer, Bullen, Boorman, Dean, Palmer.*
136	Another source has better batting orders, though probably that of dismissal. Hampshire: Small jun., Aylward, Purchase, Foster, Scott, Small sen., Ring, Taylor, Mann, Freemantle, Harris. England: Brazier, T.Walker, Wells, Sueter, Crawte, H.Walker, Winchilsea, Clifford, Bullen, Beldham, Stevens. This moves Beldham to the bottom of the England order as he was not out. He certainly came in higher up, probably at No.4 or 5.*
138	The footnote says that Grover has been tentatively identified as John Septimus Grover. He was educated at Eton and he is found playing for the Old Etonians in a newly-discovered match from 1790 (it does not qualify as a 'great' match) which makes the identification less tentative.*
144	Another source has Beldham batting at No.2 for Winchilsea's XI and the other players from T.Walker to Brazier moving one place down with Bullen at 10 and Butcher at 11. This suggests that the version in the book is in dismissal order.*
151	Add Miller's initials: J.E.A.R.
196	MP 13/8 has better batting orders. Surrey: Winchilsea, T.Walker, H.Walker, Beldham, Wells, Crawte, J.Walker, Louch, Hampton, Tufton, Milsington. England: Ring, Hammond, Freemantle, Small, Bullen, Purchase, Boxall, Cumberland, Dehany, Brudenell, Harris.
240	Add Heneage's initial: E.

Pages 271-273. The 'Lost' Great Matches

In sixth line of introduction, delete 'the' between 'all of' and 'them'.

Pages 286-294. Index of players

Further research has provided extra information on some of these.

Page
286	Beeston, J., first name John, not James.
287	Boult, A., first name Abraham.
289	Goulstone, John. His surname is Gouldstone in the baptismal register.
289	Heneage, first name Edward.
291	Reynolds, F., first name Frederic, not Frederick.
291	Miller, first names John Edward Augustus Riggs.
292	Replace Rimmington, B. with Remington, Benjamin; replace Rimmington, M. with Remington, Michael; and replace Rimmington, T. with Remington, Thomas. These three corrections are based on the baptismal registers.
293	Twistleton, Hon T.J., surname Twisleton.

293   Vallance, J., first name John.
293   Vallance, P., first name Philip.
294   Wyatt, R.B., first names Richard Barnard.

Pages 295-300. Abbreviations and Sources

Page
295   Add to Bentley: by Henry Bentley.
       Add to Britcher: by Samuel Britcher.
       Add to Epps: by William Epps.
       Add to SB: by Arthur Haygarth.
295   Abbreviations: Insert between Bath C and CJ CC = Chelsmford Chronicle.
       Insert between Oracle and PbG, PA = Public Advertiser.
296   After WEP, replace Westminster Evening Post with Whitehall Evening Post.

Add the following to the list of sources for each match on pages 296-300:

page	
38	SBp8
39	HC 12/7
45	PA, SalisJ
46	RM
51	HC 3/7
55	LEP
68	Epps erroneously dated 1779
82	Contemporary printed scorecard
92	HC 14/7, MH 16/7
113	World 4/6, LC 7/6, SJC 7/6, WEP 7/6
119	World 6/8
123	MaJ 26/5
138	Cricket Statistician Autumn 2006
139	PA 14/6
140	Cricket Statistician Autumn 2006
153	MP 17/6; for MH 16/7 read 16/6
174	For Gazette 22/8 read Gazetteer
177	For Gazette 4/9 read Gazetteer
180	Cricket Statistician Autumn 2006
181	Britcher p28
187	CC
210	For SB175 read SB173
217	For SB185 read SB181
231	WDC p144 erroneously dated 1796
232	For SB195 read SB194
241	Delete WDC p146

Batting orders

It may be of interest to note that in a few matches where the score in Great Cricket Matches 1772-1800 is apparently in dismissal order, it may be possible, when we have more than one source, to establish the actual order of going in through some logical deductions. It must be made clear that there are no contemporary sources for these inferred batting orders, which have been worked out by Keith Warsop.

Page
88   Kent: Smith, Pilcher, Ring, Boxall, Aylward, Luck, Fielder, Cumberland, Darnley, Wells, Bullen. MCC: As printed.

89   Berkshire: Monk, Finch, Shackle, Gill, Lawrence, East, Quarme, Ray, Carter, Thompson,
      Timber. MCC: Winchilsea, Louch, Bedster, Newman, Dehany, Hussey, Cumberland,
      Nicoll, Fitzroy, Tufton, Littler.
190   MCC: Beldham, Walker, Wells, Winchilsea, Fitzroy, J.Tufton, Louch, Wyatt, Newman,
      Brudenell, H.J.Tufton. Kent: As printed.
191   MCC: Wells, Hampton, Winchilsea, Beldham, Walker, Fennex, Newman, Brudenell,
      H.J.Tufton, J.Tufton, Fitzroy. Kent: As printed.
192   Winchilsea's XI: T.Walker, J.Walker, Ring, H.Walker, Winchilsea, Smith, J.Tufton,
      Dehany, H.J.Tufton, Bullen, Hampton. Louch's XI: Goldham, Aylward, Purchase,
      Freemantle, Fennex, Louch, Butcher, Boxall, Newman, Lord, Graham.

Taking as an example Winchilsea's XI on page 192 of Great Cricket Matches, note that the score, in dismissal order, is from the Sporting Magazine. This version is also in Britcher though here the amateurs have been moved up to the top, above the professionals. However, in Bentley, the amateurs are also at the top but, ignoring this for the moment, and looking just at the professionals, we see that Bentley has them in the order of going in, not of dismissal. The specialist batsmen come first and the tail-enders and bowlers come last. Note that T.Walker is first (among the professionals) and is not out 53 in a total of 90. If we take him as opening the innings, as we must if the Bentley order is to make sense, then we must realise that for the other ten players, the order of going in is also that of dismissal.

By listing the professionals in the order in which they appear in the SM we see that it exactly matches Bentley. By using the SM dismissal order we can see where the amateurs batted and have the order we give above. This tends to confirm, as all versions of the score strongly imply, that T.Walker did indeed carry his bat through this innings.

A similar procedure has been used in those four other matches on pp.188-191 where we have given a deduced batting order.